D0143574

Booker T. Washington
and the
Negro's Place
in American Life

Samuel R. Spencer, Jr.

Booker T. Washington

and the

Negro's Place
in American Life

Edited by Oscar Handlin

HarperCollins*Publishers*

ISBN 0-673-39352-6

To my mother

Editor's Preface

THE FIFTEENTH AMENDMENT brought to an end the long night of the Negroes' slavery. But emancipation was only the first dawning of their freedom; high noon would be decades in the coming. Hence their predicament as incomplete men and citizens. Hence the nation's dilemma in the face of a persistent inequality contrary to every article of its democratic faith.

When the Civil War closed, the Negroes of the South emerged from the shackled bondage that had long been their lot on this continent. But as the excitement of the first reconstruction years waned, the freedmen discovered they lacked the means to give full meaning to their liberty. Without education, skill, land, or capital they were incapable of seizing the opportunities of their society, and deep racial prejudices consigned them to a permanently inferior place in it. Held to the lowest forms of labor, cut off from the whites by the system of segregation, and devoid of political power, the Negroes seemed condemned to a hopeless servitude that made a mockery of legal emancipation.

Yet these were men and Americans, not the mere subjects of the will of others, but capable of acting on their own behalf. It was painfully difficult, given the tragic obstacles in the way, to work out a constructive policy through which the group would advance. Slowly and with difficulty, but with mounting power as the years went by, the Negroes found their leaders and picked their way toward a constructive policy that would earn them respect and, ultimately, equality.

Booker T. Washington lived through the most critical years of these developments. Born a slave, he passed his young manhood amidst the bitterest trials of the reconstruction period. The means by which he acquired an education and climbed to a position from which he could lead his fellows form themselves a dramatic and exciting story. His practical work as administrator and educator is also large with interest. But the broader implications of his life lie in the attitudes he nurtured, attitudes which explained their situation to the Negroes and at the same time pointed to the means by which they could improve it.

Washington argued it was vain for the Negro to attempt to make the full leap to equality at once. Better, he urged, to leave for the future demands for political and social power — in any case unreal at the moment — and instead to direct every energy toward raising the economic standards of the Negro. This gospel of work and training inspired Washington's own labors in behalf of the education of the group. It also gave many Negroes the beginnings of faith that although their lot for the present was miserable, there was an alternative to despair — hope that their own efforts might be rewarded with improvement.

In the closing years of his career, Washington's enemies were charging that he had outlived his times. He was no longer undisputed leader of the group; its aspirations were now taking shape in the bolder longings of younger men, born free, who had never known the realities of slavery as Washington had. There was some measure of justice to these accusations. Having become respectable and powerful, the man whose first home was a slave's cabin grew more disposed to look backward at the distance he had come than to look ahead at the way there yet remained to go.

But that only revealed that Washington was, after all, a man of his times. In this story, superbly told by Samuel R. Spencer, Jr., the living personality of the man lends meaning to one of the great issues of his times.

OSCAR HANDLIN

Contents

Booker T. Washington
and the
Negro's Place
in American Life

I

The Wilderness of Freedom

ON THE Fourth of July, 1881, thirty Negro students enrolled as the first class of a new school in Tuskegee, Alabama. The appearance of the institution belied its somewhat ambitious name, for the Tuskegee Normal and Industrial Institute boasted only two buildings, an old church and a dilapidated shanty. Both were on loan. The shanty was particularly "well ventilated," for some of its windows were ill-fitting wooden shutters on leather hinges, while others had sashes from which the glass had long since gone. The intellectual equipment of the students was no more impressive than the physical plant; while most had come with a genuine desire to learn, practically all of them considered learning an escape from the manual labor to which Negroes in the South had been and still were accustomed.

But the school had one asset which more than balanced its obvious liabilities: it had as teacher and principal Booker T. Washington, whose energy and persistence successfully defied poor students, poorer facilities, and a lamentable lack of money. Washington had arrived in the town a month before. Taken aback to find the school to which he had been called from Virginia nonexistent except for a small appropriation from the legislature for teachers' salaries, he had immediately adapted his program to meet the situation. If there were no school, he would create one. If there were no students, he would seek them out. After arranging to use the church and shanty, he spent the month of June tramping the hot countryside to learn the conditions of Negro families and to advertise Tuskegee Institute. The school opened as scheduled. That Washington chose Independence Day was completely in keeping with his flair for the dramatic.

The new institution had been founded through a mixture of altruism and self-interest. Lewis Adams, the leading Negro citizen of Tuskegee, had learned the trades of tinsmithing, shoemaking, and harness making as a slave; when free, he had built up a successful hardware and leather business. Adams was eager for a school which would give Negroes not only "book learning" but a means toward bettering their economic condition. With Colonel W. F. Foster, a former slaveholder now angling for the Negro vote in his campaign for the legislature, Adams secured from the lawmakers an annual appropriation of $2000 to pay instructional salaries of an industrial school for freedmen in Tuskegee. Other than appointing a board of commissioners, the legislature made no practical provision for the infant institution.

The commissioners took their charge seriously. In their search for a man who could direct the school they wrote to General Samuel Armstrong, principal of Hampton Institute in Virginia, the best known of the industrial schools established for the Negro after the war. They had in mind a white man. General Armstrong replied that he had no white man to recommend, but that he could and would strongly endorse Booker T. Washington, a young Negro member of his staff. The commissioners wired back: "Booker T. Washington will suit us. Send him at once."

Washington, in Virginia, could not even locate Tuskegee on the map. On inquiry he learned that it lay in the heart of the Alabama Black Belt, so called originally because of its rich dark earth, later because of its overwhelming Negro population. The Montgomery and West Point Railroad passed it by five miles to the north, but a stage ran to Tuskegee from Chehaw, the nearest station. The town numbered about 2000 souls, equally divided between whites and Negroes.

Tuskegee was the seat of Macon County, carved out of the territory ceded by the Creeks to the United States Government in 1832 and named for Nathaniel Macon, onetime Speaker of the House and President of the United States Senate. As the plantation system had spread westward to the gulf states in the decades before the Civil War, the rich land of Macon County attracted a society of prosperous slave-owning planters.

Located on a high ridge noted for its healthful qualities, the crossroads village of Tuskegee became the center of this society. Its citizens prided themselves on a tradition of education, at least for the planter class, and boasted, before the war, several academies. A women's college founded in 1845 was still thriving when Washington arrived in 1881. The fact that a public school for Negroes existed prior to the opening of Tuskegee Institute testified to some local concern for education of the former slaves.

As in most of the South, however, educational standards were low at best, and Negro schools, like the Negroes themselves, were unwanted stepchildren. The white South, decimated by the war and drained of its human and physical resources, had more than enough problems after 1865. A new social and economic system had to be built on the ruins of the plantation society which invading Union armies had swept away. Families were scattered, land titles in dispute. Planters large and small had to adjust to a free-labor system and work out an arrangement which, in the absence of ready money, would keep food on the table of both employer and employee. To make matters more confusing, the South was trying to restore an agricultural system — which was all it knew — at a time when the rest of the nation was rapidly undergoing the process of industrialization. Prewar political patterns had suffered convulsions from which they would never fully recover.

Touching and complicating each of these problems was the problem of the freedman. Of the nation's Negroes, three fourths lived in the South, most of them on farms or in small towns. When Washington went to Tuskegee, the black stepchildren of the South could see little hope and less promise in their future. Catapulted briefly into legislative chambers and governors' mansions during Reconstruction, the Negro was struggling fifteen years later to maintain a hold on the ballot, and was fast losing his grip. Economically the freedmen were little better off than before Lee's surrender, for though many, in the first flush of freedom, had left the plantations for the towns, most had remained on the farms as virtual slaves to the sharecrop and crop-lien systems. Those who had learned trades before the war faced increasing competition from white men. Abandoned by Northern friends, the freedman was helpless in the face of a sweeping tide of legal restrictions which relegated him to second-class citizenship.

The Southern states had first adjusted to the new status of the Negro through laws similar to the Black Codes of ante-bellum days. Under President Johnson's "home-rule" policy of 1865 and 1866, the white South tried to keep the freedmen strictly within bounds. State legislatures gave employers rigid control over their employees, imposing heavy penalties for vagrancy or breach of a labor contract. Negroes were restricted as to the purchase or rental of property. They could not carry firearms and in many communities had to observe a strict curfew. Such laws clearly demonstrated that the white South and the white North thought of the Negro in entirely different terms.

Congressional leaders had no sympathy with this type of legislation. In 1866, already completely at odds with President Johnson, they passed over his veto a Civil Rights Act to protect the freedmen. Then, accepting the revived Black Codes and rejection of the Fourteenth Amendment as evidence that the South still harbored the spirit of rebellion, they set out to reconstruct the wayward sisters in sterner fashion. In the Reconstruction Act of 1867, Congress divided the South into military districts, ordered conventions called in each state on the basis of universal suffrage to write new constitutions, and prescribed ratification of the Fourteenth Amendment as the *sine qua non* of readmission to the Union.

Thus began the brief period in which Negroes played an active part in the government of the Southern states. Many freedmen held positions of responsibility. South Carolina had two Negro governors, and in Mississippi,

Louisiana, Alabama, and Florida Negroes held such offices as lieutenant governor, superintendent of education, and secretary of state. Hiram Revels and Blanche K. Bruce, both of Mississippi, served in the United States Senate, and a number of Negro citizens became members of the House of Representatives.

To white Southerners it made little difference that Negro legislators often accepted the leadership of the whites, for carpetbag and Negro rule were equally odious. Nor did it matter that the Negro was not primarily responsible for the waste and incompetence, the venality and corruption of the period; he symbolized the perversion of proper standards in government and had to be returned to his proper place.

At its crudest, the determination of the white South to put the bottom rail back on the bottom took form in the night raidings, floggings, and murders of the Ku Klux Klan and the Knights of the White Camellia. On another level, Southern conservatives set out to recapture political leadership. Despite the Union League and the presence of federal troops and Northern "missionaries," the Republicans were unable to build a stable, permanent party in the South. In 1871 the "ironclad" oath required of Southern voters was repealed; 1872 brought an amnesty to all but six hundred high-ranking Confederate officials. Aided by these measures, Southern "Redeemers" regained control in every former Confederate state except South Carolina, Louisiana, and Florida; and after the election of Hayes in 1876, the last Yankee soldier packed his kit and moved northward, leaving the governments in the hands of local residents.

The short-lived attempt to make the Negro a permanent force in Southern politics was little more successful than the parallel effort of federal authorities to minister to his physical well-being. The problem of caring for thousands of displaced Negroes had begun to plague army commanders during the war. While most slaves had stayed on their home plantations during the fighting, thousands had slipped away to a haven within the Northern lines. The end of the war aggravated the situation; the exhausted South was unable to support a drifting population of four million Negroes, especially since many former slaves fully expected "Marse Lincum's" government to supply them with the necessities of life — or at least with forty acres and a mule.

The Freedmen's Bureau, set up during the war, helped tide the region over the difficulties of the period. It distributed several million rations, the majority to Negroes, but many to whites; it resettled countless freedmen cut adrift from traditional moorings, negotiated thousands of labor contracts, and tried to educate the Negroes to the importance of living up to these arrangements. It made available legal aid and planted the seeds of Negro schools throughout the South.

At best, however, the Freedmen's Bureau was a temporary panacea, for its attempts at rehabilitation did not solve the long-range problem of economic adjustment. Faced with the necessity for establishing a new pattern of livelihood, the South black and white worked out the only arrangements practicable at the time. Lack of capital made sharecropping an obvious solution in an agricultural economy. Sharecropping in turn led to the crop-lien system, under which the cropper pledged his future harvest to the local merchant. All participants were to a greater or lesser extent prisoners of this system, with the Negro as its worst victim.

Many Negroes tried to escape. Great numbers joined the westward movement, but farm distress in the last decades of the century turned them back. Others, and particularly those who had learned trades during plantation days, made their way to Northern cities or Southern towns, only to find Negroes unwanted in an increasing number of occupations. Though the idealistic and unstable Knights of Labor, which flourished during the 1880's, welcomed them, most unions in the American Federation of Labor did not. The great majority of colored men, lacking the training, initiative, and resources to find constructive solutions for their dilemma, remained sharecroppers or farmhands who lived in one-room cabins on a diet of fatback, corn bread, and black-eyed peas.

Facing an increasingly bleak prospect politically and economically, the Negro had little defense against other measures which completed his relegation to a subordinate status. In 1870 Tennessee passed a law against intermarriage, and all the other former Confederate states quickly followed. By 1875 there had begun the long procession of laws to bar Negro citizens from white hotels, restaurants, and theaters, and to require for them separate schools and separate accommodations on common carriers. In 1876 leadership in the Republican party passed to an element much more anxious to co-operate with Southern conservatives than to battle for Negro rights. When, in 1883, the Supreme Court declared the Civil Rights Act of 1875 unconstitutional, many Negroes felt themselves deserted. The last years of the century found the former slaves unorganized and untrained, "ignorant and poverty-stricken, but with a strong desire for education and the possession of property; more or less demoralized and discouraged; as suspicious and distrustful of their own race as of the white race; and, in the main, following no especially constructive leadership."

However discouraging, the situation was not hopeless. Frederick Douglass, the Negro abolitionist, was still on the scene to protest the new disabilities, and his very presence reminded Negroes of the kind of leadership they had produced and could produce again. With all their faults, hundreds of Negro schools established by the Freedmen's Bureau and missionary enterprises were still struggling along, though offering more promise for the future than answer to the present. A small stream of teachers, inadequately equipped but teachers nevertheless, was trickling out of such institutions as Atlanta, Hampton, and Fisk. On their own initiative the former slaves had also organized groups which were to serve for some time as the central agencies for concerted action: the Negro churches. With their roots in the early years of the nineteenth century, such churches as the African Methodist Episcopal and the Baptist mushroomed into national organizations, while other independent Negro churches also made rapid gains.

But the development of most significance for the future of the American Negro had to do with a single individual whom the circumstances of these years shaped for leadership. Born a slave on a Virginia plantation in 1856, a small boy who knew only the name Booker moved with his mother and stepfather to West Virginia in the great shifting of Negro population which took place immediately after the Civil War. There, working in the mines during the day and studying at night, he added the name Washington. By 1872 his ambition for an education took him to Hampton Institute. In 1881, when he made the long journey from West Virginia to Alabama to begin his life work at Tuskegee, Booker Washington could look back on twenty-five years filled with turbulence and hardship for himself as well as for his race.

Boyhood: Plantation and Salt Mine

On a midsummer day of 1860 a federal census taker rode down the slope of a Virginia hillside toward the little cluster of log buildings on the plantation of James Burroughs. He was covering the northeast district of Franklin County, a few miles east of the county seat, Rocky Mount, not far from the site of the future city of Roanoke. At the top of his census sheet he had written "Halesford," the name of the one-store post office where the Burroughs family and their neighbors called for their mail.

The plantation he approached, which was valued at about $3000, could boast little of the romance often attributed to the dwellings of Southern planters. The Burroughs residence, a two-story log house with two large rooms on each floor, faced northward up the slope and was pocketed between two knobby hills which cut off the view of the nearby Blue Ridge Mountains. Only a few feet away stood two slave cabins, also of logs, one of which served as the plantation kitchen.

On the surrounding hillsides James Burroughs and his sons, working in the field with their few slaves, raised wheat and corn and a few head of livestock. Maintenance was generally slack. A broken windowpane went for weeks without repair, fences were often down, grass and weeds grew in the yard. The furnishings of the house suggested their back-country origin; the chairs were either Windsors or split-back, and trundlebeds accommodated the constant progression of children through the years. Still, by the standards of the time and section, James Burroughs, his wife Elizabeth, and their family of thirteen children lived well enough as respected members of their community.

With his slaves Burroughs enjoyed the intimate association of the small back-country plantation. The two cabins were close enough to be almost a part of the "big house," and the master's children played with the small Negroes. Burroughs, who did not own enough Negroes to employ an overseer, treated his slaves well; a whipping was an unusual event which made a deep impression. The census taker of 1860 carefully listed the black population of the plantation: two women, aged forty and forty-one; a young man of twenty-two; and four children, a girl of twelve, an infant girl of one, and two mulatto boys, ages eight and four. The four-year-old boy, born on April 5, 1856, to the plantation cook, Jane, was known as Booker.

Jane Burroughs's husband was a slave named Washington Ferguson, who belonged to a neighboring family and visited the Burroughs place only infrequently. Of her three children, only one, the infant daughter three years younger than Booker, was his child. Booker's brother John, four years older than he, was the mulatto boy of eight noted by the census taker. Who his own father was Booker never learned, other than that he was a white man from a nearby plantation; but the parentage of slave children, to that place and time, was often irrelevant.

Booker spent his first nine years in the cabin which doubled as the plantation kitchen, the memory of which stayed with him in detail all his life. A rectangular box 16 by 14 feet, it had a tremendous fireplace at one end at which Jane did the cooking for both whites and Negroes. Booker welcomed the open fire during the months when the wind whistled in through the window openings and the ineffective door, but in the summer it made the cabin almost unbearable. Since there was little or no furniture, Booker and the other two children slept on the earthen floor on ragged pallets.

Booker and his brother ate where and when they could. When their mother left early for her duties at the "big house," they usually made a breakfast from the boiled corn set out for the cows and pigs. At other times Booker "came into possession" of one or two potatoes from the "potato hole" in the floor of the cabin; these he roasted in the ashes of the open fire. Sometimes, late at night, his mother would awaken her children for a feast of chicken or eggs which she had cooked for them "undercover." But the greatest treat of all was the weekly offering of molasses from the big house. Booker eagerly held up his tin plate for this cherished ration, tilting the surface back and forth to spread the molasses and "make it go farther."

Until he was quite large, his only garment was a long shirt made of flax. New flaxen shirts were rough and sticky, a near torture to a sensitive skin until "broken in." On several occasions his older brother John wore the roughness off a new shirt for him — an early indication of a characteristic spirit of generosity. Because the shoes given them to wear had inflexible wooden soles, the children went barefoot most of the time when it was not too cold.

Like other slave children, Booker received his share of the plantation chores. He sometimes operated a system of paper fans which slid back and forth on ropes and pulleys to keep the flies off the master's dining table; on occasion, he held the horses of the Burroughs daughters when they went riding with guests. As he grew older, his master entrusted to him the more important task of taking corn to the mill to be ground, but stories of army deserters who caught Negro boys and cut off their ears made this duty a somewhat uneasy one, especially since it often kept him away from home until after dark.

Since the Civil War began when Booker was only five years old, most of his plantation memories were of the war years. He later recalled the keen interest of the Negroes in the war despite the fact that not a slave on the plantation could read. Their loyalties were divided. A simple human affection for the Burroughs family and a larger identification with the interests of the people and section they knew vied with the partly intuitive conviction that their own interests lay with the Northern armies. When "Marse Billy," James Burroughs's son, went off to war and was killed, the mourning in the slave quarters was genuine. Two other sons came home wounded, and the slaves contested for the privilege of caring for them. When the family silver was buried to hide it from the invading Yankees, not a single slave would have betrayed the secret; and they stood ready to defend with their lives the women of the family entrusted to their care.

Still, they rejoiced at the news of every success of the Union armies. The slave who went for the mail gleaned from small talk at the general store every shred of information available and passed it on to his fellow slaves at the plantation. Booker drank in not only current news, but other kinds of information as well. He learned something of how his forebears were taken into slavery; how they often died in the notorious "middle passage" from the homeland to America; and how all of them longed for the day of "jubilo" when freedom and all its blessings would come. One of his earliest impressions resulted from being awakened late one night by the prayer of his mother, kneeling beside him, that some day she and her children would be free.

As the war dragged on through the weary years of 1864 and 1865, the privations of both whites and Negroes increased. An ersatz coffee was made from parched corn, molasses took the place of sugar, and other imported items of food and clothing disappeared from general use. The Negro, whose usual diet of salt pork and corn bread was raised on the plantation, felt the pinch less than the whites. As the Confederate armies reached the point of exhaustion, increasing numbers of deserters, disillusioned and weary, passed the Burroughs plantation on their way home. Freedom was in the air, and in the "quarters" the slaves sang more openly of the great day of release from bondage. When word came that something unusual would happen the next day, every slave on the plantation knew what it meant.

There was little sleep in the slave cabins that night. The following morning all the Negroes, young and old, gathered at the big house. where all the members of the

Burroughs family then at home waited on the porch. A government official read the Emancipation Proclamation and explained that the slaves were free to go where they pleased. Booker remembered that there was no bitterness on the part of the master's family, but rather a sadness at the end of the only kind of life they had known.

Momentarily, great exultation reigned among the slaves. By the time they returned to their cabins, however, the weight of responsibility had begun to settle on their shoulders. They were free, but free to do what? They had no place to go, few skills with which to earn a living, no experience in managing their own affairs. One by one, in a scene repeated on thousands of Southern plantations, they made their way quietly to the big house to ask their former owners what to do.

For Jane Burroughs the decision was made by her husband, Washington Ferguson. During the war Ferguson had escaped from his home plantation and settled in the little town of Malden, five miles from Charleston, West Virginia. He now sent a wagon to bring his wife, her children, and their meager belongings on the two-hundred-mile journey across the mountains. After many days of travel they reached their new home in the valley of the Kanawha River.

The new surroundings were even more primitive and less adequate than the slave cabin they had left behind. Malden was a shabby, crowded community clustered near the salt mines, for the production of salt was the chief industry of the region. At the mines Washington Ferguson had found work as a packer. Up to that time Ferguson had meant little or nothing to Booker, who had seen him only on Christmas and other special occasions when he visited the Burroughs plantation. The fact that they now became members of the same household for seven years did not change the situation materially, for Ferguson's lack of ambition and improvidence as a husband and father did not earn him the respect of his nine-year-old stepson.

The relationship between the boy and his mother was another story. Though only a slave woman, she was to him the "noblest embodiment of womanhood." Her surreptitious acquisition of her master's eggs and chickens for her children during plantation days Booker stanchly excused as a concomitant of the system into which she had been born. He maintained that after they were free, no one more vigorously upheld standards of integrity and honesty than did his mother. She was endowed with an abundant fund of common sense, and, considering her environment, with extraordinary ambition for her children. Undoubtedly she recognized Booker as an exceptional child and sympathized with his longing for a better life than she was able to offer him.

Still, it would have taken more than Jane Burroughs's sympathy and ambition to transform the hovel now occupied by her family into anything like a real home. Overshadowed by a high railroad embankment at the front door, the cabin was one of a miserable collection of crowded dwellings where filth, ignorance, poverty, and immorality prevailed. Since segregation practices had not by that time crystallized into law or even into tradition, Negroes and dissolute whites lived together. The complete absence of sanitation produced an ever-present stench over the entire area.

Despite their poverty, Jane's heart went out to a child in the community who had been left without parents.

Adopted into the household and given the name James, he became an accepted member of the family. James was younger than both John, then thirteen, and Booker, who was nine, but all three boys soon went to work at the salt mines with their foster father. The mines were wells drilled deep into the earth to tap pools of salt water which pumps brought to the surface. As it came up, the water was boiled away in huge receptacles, leaving a residue of wet salt at the bottom. After being spread out on large platforms to dry, the salt was packed into barrels.

Ferguson's task as a packer was to beat the salt into the barrels until they reached the required weight. To this labor the boys contributed as much as they could. Each packer was assigned a number, and Booker's first reading lesson came in learning to recognize the figure 18 as it was chalked onto the barrels which Ferguson and his stepsons packed during the course of each day.

Even as a child Booker had enough discernment to see that education was the key to further advancement. During his first year in Malden he met a young Negro from Ohio who could read the newspapers, an achievement which immediately set the young man apart from his fellows. As the Negro population gathered eagerly around the scholar to hear him read the news of the day, Booker watched in envious admiration, determined that nothing would prevent him from acquiring this remarkable gift. To his profound satisfaction his mother managed to pick up for him a copy of Webster's blueback speller, and this soon enabled him to master the alphabet.

Self-education only whetted the boy's appetite for more. Already there was a demand among the Negro population of Malden for a school, not simply for the children, but for their parents and even for gray-haired grandmothers and grandfathers who wanted most to read the Bible for themselves before they died. About this time a tall, light-skinned Negro war veteran named William Davis arrived in the community from Ohio and was hired as a teacher. Those who attended school pooled their meager resources to offer a small cash salary, board, and room. Each family entertained the teacher in turn on a "boarding 'round" arrangement, and since the presence of a guest called for special effort on the part of the family cook, Booker looked forward with an "anxious appetite" to the teacher's day in his home.

To his bitter disappointment, he was at first denied the privilege of going to school because his labor in the mines was too valuable. Refusing to give up, he embarked on a determined campaign to break down Ferguson's resistance. His stepfather finally agreed that Booker might attend the school, but only on the condition that he put in five hours at the mine between four in the morning and nine, and an additional two hours after school in the afternoon. This hard bargain Booker accepted.

At school Booker adopted the name by which he was identified the rest of his life. During the roll call he noticed that all his schoolmates had at least two names, and that several of them indulged in the luxury of three. Though he himself had known nothing but Booker, he was equal to the occasion when the time came. Asked for his name, he answered without hesitation, "Booker Washington." Later he explained that he had cast about for the grandest name he could think of; then, too, Washington was the name by which his stepfather was commonly known. Whatever the origin of the idea, Booker Washington he was from that day on. Later, learning that his mother had given him at birth the name Taliaferro, he restored it also, making his full name Booker Taliaferro Washington.

One other thing was lacking: unlike the rest of the children, he had no hat. This he reported to his mother, who told him she had no money to buy a "store hat" but promised to do what she could. With two pieces of homespun, a needle, and thread, she fashioned a hat which satisfied the need. The fact that his mother's common sense outweighed her desire to buy him a "store hat" for appearance's sake made a deep impression on Booker, who absorbed the lesson of thrift and lack of pretense. He noted years later that some of those who had jeered at his odd hat landed in the penetentiary, and that others eventually accomplished so little that they could afford to buy no hats at all.

Having acquired surname and hat, Booker proceeded to devour what was offered to him as rapidly as it was given. He became increasingly aware of the condition of his people, and though he could not then put his feeling into words, he reacted intuitively against his teacher's dictum that the chief end of education was to speak and write the English language correctly. Young as he was, education had for Booker a utilitarian purpose: to make life more endurable. Quite naturally, it was his mother whom he wanted most to lift from a life of hardship.

Unfortunately for such aspirations, the very poverty of the family caused his stepfather to renege on his bargain. Back to work Booker went, this time to the nearby coal mines which furnished fuel for the salt furnaces. At first he and his brothers served as trappers, regulating the flow of air into the mine by alternately opening and closing trap doors at the end of the mine shafts. As he grew older, Booker learned to swing a pick down in the dark recesses of the mine itself. He loathed the work. He could never learn his way through the subterranean rooms and trembled with fear when the light on his cap went out. Accidents were common, and Booker despised the dirt in which he labored.

For more than five years, from 1865 to 1871, Ferguson's stepsons worked alternately in the salt and coal mines. Booker studied whenever he could, snatching intervals to pore over his speller by the light of his miner's lamp. His mother continued to help by arranging to have him taught at night, though often he walked several miles for a lesson only to find that the teacher knew less than he.

One day in the coal mine an overheard conversation gave him a tangible goal, one which he kept before him like the tiny pinpoint of light at the opening of the mine shaft. Two miners working near him spoke of a school in eastern Virginia established for the express purpose of teaching Negroes trades. Moving nearer, Booker heard that the school offered work opportunities for those who could not pay their way. Though he did not know where the school was or how to get there, Booker did learn its name: Hampton Institute. At that moment he resolved that, come what might, he would eventually go to Hampton.

Early in 1871 he and his mother heard that Mrs. Viola Ruffner, the wife of General Lewis Ruffner, owner of the mines, wanted a houseboy to live at her home. Booker, by that time fifteen, knew very well Mrs. Ruffner's reputation as a hyperstrict Yankee woman whom no one could please and had no desire to become one of the succession of boys who had tried the place and left. Still, compared with the coal mines even Mrs. Ruffner seemed the lesser of evils, and with some misgivings he allowed his mother to apply in his behalf. Mrs. Ruffner hired him at six dollars per month and room and meals.

For the following year and a half he received a most exacting practical education. By no means a model employee at first, he seemed destined to follow the pattern of his predecessors. One of his first tasks was to cut the front lawn with a hand scythe. He finished the job, only to be told the work was not satisfactory. Again he went over the yard on his hands and knees, and again it would not do. Only after two more trimmings was Mrs. Ruffner satisfied. His taskmistress would tolerate not a single speck of dirt, not a single grease spot, not a tool or implement out of place. Awed and discouraged, Booker decided to run away; he did not, however, go home. Since Malden was on the Great Kanawha River near its junction with the Ohio, steamboats still made their way between that point and Cincinnati. Approaching the captain of one of these boats, Booker secured a job as a waiter, only to demonstrate at the first meal that he was totally unfit for the task. Though the captain fired him without ceremony, the runaway's powers of persuasion enabled him to cajole his erstwhile employer into taking him on to Cincinnati and back to Malden. This abortive enterprise was Booker's first view of the world beyond the Burroughs plantation and the Malden mines.

Contrite in spirit, he made his way back to Mrs. Ruff-

ner. Allowed to return, he adjusted himself to the situation and made the most of his opportunities. After restor-
ing himself to her good graces, he was permitted to go
to school during the afternoons; when this occasionally
proved impracticable, he resorted again to night lessons
from private teachers. Mrs. Ruffner encouraged him in
his desire for education, and it was at her home that he
made shelves out of a dry-goods box, collected any and all
books he could lay his hands on, and set up his first "library."

Mrs. Ruffner also provided him with his first business
experience. Since she raised in her garden fruits and vegetables for sale to other families in the community, she
often sent Booker out with a large basket to make the
rounds from house to house. Gifted in his relations with
people, Booker enjoyed this venture into the world of
commerce despite the fact that he often had to stand off
other boys who tried to wheedle or intimidate him into
parting with some of his wares. As receipts from his sales
mounted, with every penny accounted for, Mrs. Ruffner
lost any doubts she may have had as to his honesty or
ability. For his part, as he learned the value of her exacting standards of performance, his pride in a job well done
developed into a major incentive. From that time on, the
gospel of thrift, propriety, cleanliness and hard work
which was Mrs. Ruffner's New England heritage also became a part of the young Negro's make-up.

The association with Mrs. Ruffner was not, however,
the kind of education on which he had set his heart, and
he never dropped the idea of going to Hampton. Though
his mother had misgivings about his wandering so far
from home — she had been in poor health for some time

and was afraid she would be telling him good-by for the last time — she continually encouraged him in his ambition. Mrs. Ruffner, too, gave him her blessing.

Finally, in the fall of 1872, he determined to make the break. Though almost all of his earnings had gone into the family pocketbook, he had managed to save a little. His brother John, generous as always, gave what he could from his own meager earnings. Other small contributions came from well-wishers in the community, especially from the older people, for the departure of one of their race for boarding school was a novel and meaningful event. Despite this interest, his total resources amounted to a mere pittance. This he hoped would cover his travel expenses, though he had no conception of the distance to Hampton or of the cost of public transportation, food, and accommodations.

From Malden through the mountains and across the state of Virginia was a distance of some four hundred miles. No railroads had found their way west of Lynchburg, and the first hundred miles or so had to be covered by stagecoach. Wearing his only suit and carrying a cheap little satchel with a change of underwear, the sixteen-year-old Negro boy climbed aboard the stage in Malden. For the first time he learned what it meant to have a dark skin when, at the end of the day, the stagecoach pulled up at an unpainted frame house advertised as a hotel. Booker assumed that rooms were available for all passengers. Respectfully, after waiting until the last white passenger had received a room assignment from the clerk, he stepped up to the desk. Not only was there no bed available for him; he was allowed neither to remain in the building nor to buy any food. He spent most of the night walking about to keep warm, boarding the stage again the next morning weary from hunger and lack of sleep.

Somewhere in northern Virginia his money gave out. For the rest of the way he walked and begged rides. Finally, late one night, dirty, famished, and tired, he reached Richmond. His first thought was to find a place to sleep, but even his gifts of persuasion could not overcome the disadvantage of having no money to offer. Never having been in a city before, and knowing no one, he walked the streets aimlessly, his mouth watering at the sight of fried chicken and half-moon apple pies piled high on the food stands. Near exhaustion, he arrived at a place where a wooden sidewalk was elevated enough to offer shelter beneath. Waiting until he was sure no one would see him, he slipped under the sidewalk and lay down with his satchel as a pillow. The tramp of feet above his head was not enough to overcome his weariness, and he slept until morning.

Emerging from his improvised bedroom, he found himself at the waterfront, near a ship loading pig iron. Seeing that he was ravenously hungry, the captain agreed to let him work enough to earn money for breakfast — the best breakfast, he said later, of his entire life. His employer was so impressed with the boy's work that he offered to hire him indefinitely, an offer which Booker gladly accepted. Continuing to sleep under the sidewalk to save money, he worked at the ship until he had saved enough to take him the remaining eighty-two miles to Hampton.

I I I

Hampton: Book Learning and Hero Worship

LOCATED on the famous peninsula between the York and the James rivers, Hampton Institute in the autumn of 1872 centered in Academic Hall, an imposing three-story brick building completed only the year before. To the untraveled and untutored Negro boy from West Virginia it was the largest and most beautiful structure imaginable. Except, however, for Academic Hall and the "mansion house" of the former plantation on which the school was built, the four-year-old institute boasted little physical equipment.

Its staff was headed by the founder and principal, General Samuel C. Armstrong, who had grown up in Hawaii as the son of missionaries. Armstrong first came to the United States in 1860 to enter Williams College, where his fellow students recognized immediately an influence "as fresh and strong as an island breeze." "His constitution smacked of the seas," one of them wrote. "It seemed natural for him to strike out in any element."

This remarkable youth, a trifle above average height, broad-shouldered, browned by the sun and wind, with deep-set, flashing eyes, fell immediately under the spell of President Mark Hopkins, in whose home he lived. While he was at Williams, Fort Sumter was fired upon and the war began. More a Hawaiian than an American, Armstrong was not deeply moved at first. This feeling soon changed, however, and immediately upon graduation in 1862 (he had entered as a junior) he declared himself "in for the army." Hastening to Troy, New York, he pitched a tent in a public square and began to campaign for recruits in the surrounding towns. Meanwhile he studied tactics, and when he had enlisted the required one hundred men in his company, he was sworn in as a captain and assigned to the One Hundred and Twenty-fifth New York Regiment.

The young captain's first military venture was a fiasco, for his regiment arrived at Harpers Ferry, Virginia, just in time to join twelve thousand other Federal troops who were bagged by Stonewall Jackson. Shipped back to a parole camp, Armstrong and his company remained idle for months. His chance for action finally came at Gettysburg, where he won a promotion to major. During the war he became seriously interested in the Negro, and by 1864 the Union was little to him: "I see only the four million slaves, and for them I fight." On his own application he was assigned to duty with Negro troops for the rest of the war. By the late spring of 1865, when he and his unit were shipped to the Mexican border for a brief period of service, he had become a brevet brigadier general at the age of twenty-six.

Discharged from the army, he applied for a position with the newly organized Freedmen's Bureau and ultimately was offered direction of the fifth subdistrict of Virginia, covering ten counties, with headquarters at Hampton. This was the hardest post in the state, for there were thirty-five thousand former slaves in his area, and seven thousand within a three-mile radius of his office. For two years he worked to solve the manifold problems of this great army of displaced persons. Through philanthropic agencies in the North he placed nearly one thousand as domestic servants, meanwhile attempting to relocate thousands of others or give them training to make them self-sufficient.

Increasingly, however, looking upon the Bureau as a mere palliative, he became convinced that a well-organized educational system offered the only long-term solution for the freedmen. Many times his mind went back to the manual-labor school he had observed in Hawaii, where native islanders received "industrial" training for the mechanical trades. The former slaves needed, he was sure, the same kind of preparation.

With this in mind, he asked the American Missionary Association to establish a school for Negroes at Hampton. Though offered the presidency of Howard University at about the same time, he chose to become principal of the new institution. Having received contributions of almost $30,000 from wealthy Northern friends and an appropriation of $13,000 from the Freedmen's Bureau, he bought a local plantation and began operation of the school at Hampton on April 1, 1868. Two years later an independent board of trustees took over direction from the American Missionary Association, and the school was incorporated as the Hampton Normal and Agricultural Institute.

Armstrong's enthusiasm and the diligence of his staff kept the institute going. As early as 1870 he began annual tours of New York and New England to tap the reservoirs of Northern philanthropy. Well-to-do Eastern families also provided him with his faculty. In addition, General James F. B. Marshall, an old friend from Hawaii, became treasurer in 1869 as "a tail to Armstrong's kite" — a practical balance to the idealism and enthusiasm of the young founder.

From the first, Armstrong emphasized the practical and utilitarian. His avowed purpose was "to train selected Negro youths who should go out and teach and lead their people, first by example, by getting land and homes." He resolved "to give them not a dollar that they could earn for themselves," but to teach "respect for labor" and to "replace stupid drudgery with skilled hands." The mastery of "industrial" — mechanical or agricultural — skills, the development of character, and the imparting of the rudiments of learning were to move forward together. "Those who are in earnest and who come with a stout heart and two willing hands," the principal advertised in the school's first circular, "may feel that it is entirely possible for them to push their way to a good preparation for the lifework before them."

Other than the small sum of fifty cents, Booker Washington could offer literally nothing more than a stout heart and two willing hands when he applied for admission. He was one of an oversupply of applicants. "We are growing rapidly," Armstrong had written shortly before; "there is an inundation of students and we need more force." Having traveled, worked, and slept in his only suit since leaving West Virginia days before, Booker could hardly have hoped to make an impressive appearance when he presented himself to Mary Mackie, the assistant principal, for an interview. Still doubtful after having talked with him, she put him off temporarily. As hours passed and the boy saw others admitted, he became increasingly anxious. Finally he approached Miss Mackie again. "The adjoining recitation room needs sweeping," she told him. "Take the broom and sweep it."

It was a clear case of Br'er Rabbit and the briar patch. Booker could see that his entrance examination was before him, and for such an examination he was well equipped. "I knew I could sweep," he reminisced later, "for Mrs. Ruffner had taught me that art well." He went over every inch of the room three times with a broom and four times with a dust cloth, moving all the furniture and making a point of searching out the dirt in the closets. When he had finished, he reported to Miss Mackie. She went into the room, carefully inspected the floors, rubbed her handkerchief on the woodwork and the furniture. Finally she turned to the expectant Negro boy and said with a quiet smile, "I guess you will do to enter this institution."

Booker's performance with the broom also earned him a job as janitor of the building. With a characteristic seizing of opportunity he set out to make himself indispensable, proving so efficient that he soon received the full cost of his board — ten dollars a month — in return for his work. He was grateful for this despite the fact that he had to rise at four in the morning to build fires and work late at night cleaning classrooms. General Armstrong soon became interested in him and arranged for S. Griffith Morgan, of New Bedford, Massachusetts, a friend of the school, to pay his tuition fee of seventy dollars.

Despite this aid and the income from his janitorial

duties, Booker struggled constantly to make ends meet. The matter of books he solved by borrowing from those who had more money, but the problem of clothes was at first a severe trial. General Armstrong, insisting on personal cleanliness, inspected the students regularly for missing buttons, grease spots, and unpolished shoes. For a boy with one suit, one pair of socks, and a change of underwear, this standard was difficult to meet. Sympathetic teachers came to the rescue with clothing from missionary barrels sent down from the North, a source which supplied him throughout his three years at Hampton.

Among his first and strangest lessons were those which had nothing to do with books or industry. Like many of his fellow students, Booker had little knowledge of personal hygiene. Confronted with a pair of sheets on his bed, he did not know what to do. The first night he slept under both, the second night on top of both, and only after watching the seven other boys in the room did he fathom the mystery. He soon learned, too, the function of the toothbrush and the value of a bath. Convinced that the latter promoted not only health but self-respect and virtue, he made the daily bath one of the maxims by which he lived, insisting upon it even when, in later years, he had to slip away from a rural Negro cabin to a nearby stream for the purpose.

But the most meaningful experience of his first year at Hampton was his contact with General Armstrong. "The first time I went into his presence," he wrote later, "he made the impression upon me of being a perfect man." The impression did not diminish with the years, and as he looked back on his experience at Hampton, Booker consciously or unconsciously paraphrased the famous aphorism about Armstrong's own mentor Mark Hopkins: "One might have removed from Hampton all the buildings, classrooms, teachers, and industries, and given the men and women there the opportunity of coming into daily contact with General Armstrong, and that alone would have been a liberal education."

Having finished the year at Hampton owing sixteen dollars to the treasurer, Booker gave up the idea of going home for the summer when his plan for financing the trip by the sale of an old overcoat fell through. (His only prospective purchaser proposed to pay him a nickel down and the balance later.) Instead he took a job in a restaurant at nearby Fortress Monroe. Since his wages covered little more than the cost of board and lodging, he ended the summer with little to show for his time except the additional knowledge gleaned from reading and studying during leisure hours.

The treasurer let him re-enter school despite his still-outstanding debt. Though he continued to take every opportunity which came his way, life was still not easy. His janitorial duties consumed most of his spare time, and at one point he had to give up the relative comfort of the dormitory for wintry quarters in tents. The winter was cold, and Booker and his tentmates often huddled together during the nights to make maximum use of their few blankets.

Such conditions made only too obvious the need for dormitory space as the number of students, about a hundred and thirty when Booker arrived, climbed to more than two hundred. With characteristic self-confidence General Armstrong determined to build a large new dormitory which he located and named before as much as

$2000 was in hand to build it. The lack of funds did not disturb him. "The way to do," he explained to the man who was to superintend the construction, "is to plow out a hole and pile the bricks and lumber round. I'll get a party of people down from the North and make it appeal to them." Though the Panic of 1873 which paralyzed the nation's economy temporarily interrupted construction, by 1875 Virginia Hall stood among the growing cluster of buildings on the banks of the James.

Though no candidate could be admitted to Hampton unless he could read and write, the paucity of preparatory training meant that instruction was on an elementary level. During the first of three years a student took basic courses in arithmetic, English grammar, reading, spelling, geography, and natural history. Continuing his study in the three divisions of mathematics, language (English), and natural science, he added United States history in his second year, and in his third branched out into world history, civil government, and "moral sciences." The curriculum also included for all students "practical instruction in agriculture, in housework and in household industries, and drill in teaching."

Though this was the course of instruction which Booker pursued, many of his most valuable lessons did not come from books. Through the "practical instruction in agriculture" he gained a knowledge of the best breeds of stock and fowls, and throughout his life he prided himself on the animals and chickens in his own barnyard. At Hampton he developed another habit which he continued throughout life: a daily reading of the Bible. His first acquaintance with organized religion had come in Malden, where an old man upbraided him for playing marbles one

Sunday morning and persuaded him to go to Sunday School. He then joined the Baptist Church, but his understanding and love of the Bible he acquired at Hampton from two New England teachers, Nathalie Lord and Elizabeth Brewer. Under their tutelage he developed the practice of reading at least a few verses before he began work each day.

From Nathalie Lord he also learned the fundamentals of public speaking. Recognizing his talents, she spent many hours giving him lessons in breathing, emphasis, and articulation. Though he later professed a distaste for public speaking in and of itself, he sought every opportunity at Hampton to master this valuable tool. Unquestionably, too, he enjoyed the avenues it opened to him. More than any other extracurricular activity, the debating societies which met on Saturday evenings captured his interest; he never missed a meeting. Avidly interested in self-improvement, he also organized an "After Supper Club" devoted to discussion of current topics during the twenty "idle" minutes between the end of the meal and the beginning of evening study.

Money from his mother and brother and a small gift from one of the teachers at Hampton made it possible for him to look forward to a summer at home after his second year. His arrival in Malden occasioned great interest and rejoicing throughout the community. Because the people who had sent him to Hampton two years before wanted to hear about his experience to the last detail, he had to eat a meal with virtually every family. He was also in great demand as a speaker.

The pleasure of being welcomed as a returning hero soon dimmed before the hard realization that he could not find a job. He had counted on earning enough money either at the salt furnaces or the coal mines to pay his return travel and a part of the next year's expenses, but both industries were idle because of a strike. Booker had little sympathy for the workers, observing that the miners were usually worse off after the strike than before and that "professional labor agitators" had brought them little more than hardship and debts which they could not afford. Desperately, feeling that he had to have work or give up the idea of returning to Hampton, he tramped about the countryside looking for some sort of job.

He had been at home about a month when he had to face "the severest trial" he had ever experienced. On the way home one evening from a neighboring town where he had been looking for work, he became so tired that within a mile or so of Malden he stopped in the boiler room at one of the salt furnaces and went to sleep. In the early morning hours he felt a hand on his shoulder, and awoke to find his brother John there with the news that their mother had died during the night.

The rest of the summer was bleak. His sister Amanda, too young and immature to run the household, could not cope with the responsibility thrust upon her. Meals often consisted of nothing more than a can of tomatoes and crackers. Only the friendship and sympathy of his old employer, Mrs. Ruffner, provided a bright spot for the young student. The work she gave him on occasion, together with a temporary job at a nearby mine, furnished enough money for his return trip to Hampton. As usual, John also contributed — this time clothing which he somewhere managed to obtain. Toward the end of the summer Booker was further cheered by a letter from Miss Mackie asking him to be on hand before school opened to help her put the buildings in order. Eagerly accepting this invitation, he left for Hampton at once.

For two weeks he built up credit in the treasurer's office by cleaning rooms, washing windows, and making beds. It amazed him to find that Miss Mackie, with her background of Northern wealth and education, worked beside him, taking obvious satisfaction in doing well such menial tasks. Miss Mackie's lesson in the "dignity of labor" made a deep impression on him and reinforced the precepts of his first Yankee schoolteacher, Mrs. Ruffner.

During his final year at Hampton, Booker devoted himself to his studies with more than ordinary zeal, achieving his ambition to become one of the commencement speakers. He graduated in 1875 realizing that his formal training, despite its value, could not match what General Armstrong had given him by precept and example. The general, in turn, cherished an affection and regard for this favorite pupil almost equal to the pupil's hero worship for the principal. This mutual respect and admiration deepened with the years. To Washington, Armstrong was "the rarest, strongest, and most beautiful character" he had ever met — an estimate made years later when the circle of his acquaintances had widened to include more than a few notables. To Armstrong, Washington was the embodiment of what the Negro in America could hope to become.

It was only natural that Washington should have consciously and unconsciously modeled himself on his teacher and benefactor. Many legacies passed from the older man to the younger: a fine sense of integrity, a heaping measure of courage and determination, a buoyant optimism, a practical utilitarianism, and a firm self-discipline. With them came the deep-seated faith in laissez-faire individualism characteristic of the age.

For three years after his graduation Washington did what Armstrong intended every Hampton graduate to do: he became a missionary to his people, returning to Malden to take over the school which had given him his first formal education. Before he could begin, however, he had to earn enough money to pay his fare to Malden and give him a start financially, for he had finished Hampton without a cent in his pocket. Along with other students, he took a job during the summer of 1875 at the United States Hotel in Saratoga, where he made the mistake of signing on as a waiter without having a very clear conception of what a waiter in a carriage-trade hotel should know. Bungling his first assignment completely, he was reduced to the position of dishwasher, but this humiliation stimulated his determination to learn, and within a few weeks he had the satisfaction of being restored to the place for which he was originally hired.

When the season closed, he returned to Malden and dived willingly into a task which could have been infinitely discouraging. His optimism and even temperament stood him in good stead. From eight in the morning until ten at night he labored, teaching children in the day school and adults at night. His work was made easier by the eagerness of his pupils, especially the adults, but this was offset by the painfully slow pace at which many of them had to move. On Sundays he also did double duty, teaching Sunday School in the morning at Snow Hill, a community about two miles distant, and in the afternoon at Malden.

Along with academic training he imparted to his eighty or more younger students the Hampton gospel of cleanliness and order. Though the standard was almost impossible to maintain, he insisted at least in principle on clean faces, buttoned coats, and combed hair. Despite the innovations such a policy caused in many homes, he had the confidence of most of the parents, who tried to help their offspring follow instructions even when these included such luxuries as the daily bath and use of the toothbrush. Old and young attended the weekly meetings of the debating society he organized, a plan which featured debates with similar organizations in Charleston and other nearby towns. Driven by a concern for community welfare totally new to Malden, Washington became a social worker as well as a teacher.

The town could use such a person in those days. The intermingling of low-income whites and Negroes made for continuing tension, and the Ku Klux Klan functioned actively. He saw one open battle in which a hundred or so persons were engaged on each side. In this instance General Ruffner tried to intervene on behalf of the Negroes, only to be knocked down and given an injury from which he never fully recovered. Shaken by such exhibitions, Washington felt at times that there was little future for the Negro in America. But he never lost hope entirely, and he pinned his faith mainly upon giving to his race the kind of education he had learned at Hampton. One of the central purposes of his years at Malden was to prepare a few of the brighter students to enter his alma mater; he succeeded in sending four in addition to his brother John, to whom he owed a considerable debt. After John had completed the course, he and Booker made it possible for their foster brother, James, to go to Hampton also.

After three years at Malden, Washington decided to go to Wayland Seminary in Washington for a year of graduate training. Wayland's philosophy of education differed widely from that of Hampton, for it was devoted exclusively to the liberal arts. The "deep religious spirit" there, together with the "high Christian character" of the president, made a deep impression on Washington, but many things impressed him less favorably. He looked with a disapproving eye on the lack of moral fiber in the students, most of whom had their expenses paid for them. The training was not practical enough; Wayland graduates might know Latin and Greek, but they did not learn much about life as they would have to meet it. Nor did they have ingrained into them a sense of obligation to their race.

His experience at Wayland helped nurture a prejudice against purely academic training which had been rooted in Washington's mind by his education at Hampton. He acquired also a dislike for the kind of life the Negro community of the capital lived. He looked with contempt on the young Negro man-about-town who spent half a week's salary on a buggy to ride up and down Pennsylvania Avenue on Sundays, and on the young Negro government worker who could not support himself on the respectable salary of seventy-five to one hundred dollars a month. Feeling that land was the only solid basis for prosperity, he longed to transplant to the farms the many Washington Negroes who looked to the government for support.

At the end of his eight months in Washington he received an invitation which offered a completely novel experience. The fact that Wheeling, then capital of West Virginia, was located on the western edge of the state had caused considerable dissatisfaction among inhabitants of other areas. Desire for a change had culminated in a decision to move the capital, and three towns, one of them Charleston, vied for the honor. The choice was to be made by a state-wide vote. The committee for Charleston, alive to the necessity for Negro support as well as white, asked Washington to join them in stumping the state. Flattered, Washington accepted, and for three months used his persuasive powers on the voters. The decision was in favor of Charleston, a fact in which Washington allowed himself a measure of personal pride.

The exhilaration of the platform stirred a "slumbering ambition" to become a lawyer. The temptation was great, for the law offered one of the few pathways to political and economic prestige. Washington had not unnaturally thought of politics, and his success as a speaker led some of his white friends to urge a political career upon him; consequently, under the tutelage of one of these men, a Charleston attorney, he began to study law in earnest. Still, he could not banish the feeling, ill defined though it was, that to enter law or politics would run counter to all he had learned at Hampton. It looked like an escape; it lacked the element of service which he had been taught to consider fundamental.

While nagged by such doubts he received an invitation from General Armstrong to deliver the coming commencement address at Hampton. Washington worked hard on his speech, which he entitled, "The Force That Wins."

Hardly had he returned to West Virginia when another letter from General Armstrong asked him to join the Hampton staff. The general was embarking upon the experiment of bringing Indian youths from the West to Hampton in the belief that the Hampton type of training could benefit the red race as well as the black; he wanted Washington to take charge of the newcomers. To accept meant the end of the study of law. It also meant the end of his work in Malden, where he had not only served the community well but had made himself one of its most respected citizens. On the other hand, he felt that he could not refuse anything General Armstrong asked. This time, as he made the now familiar journey across the mountains, he left Malden for good.

The Hampton he went back to had progressed considerably in the four years since he had left it. The student body now numbered over three hundred, the staff had increased to twenty-four, and the indefatigable efforts of General Armstrong had brought in more than $150,000 from Northern philanthropies for capital improvements. When Bishop Potter of New York went to Hampton to lay the cornerstones of two new structures, a sudden shower threatened to delay the ceremony. "Had we not better wait?" someone asked. "Oh, no," replied the bishop. "If we wait, General Armstrong will have another cornerstone ready." The trades of shoemaking, painting, carpentering and blacksmithing had been further developed. In 1878 General Armstrong had instituted a system of military drill and inspection, explaining that the purpose was to inculcate "neatness, order, system, obedience" and thereby to make better men.

The Indian experiment came about as a result of the

Indian war which ended in 1875, when the United States Government attempted to guarantee a peaceful era in the West by transporting seventy-five chiefs and warriors to St. Augustine, Florida, for imprisonment. Fortunately their care fell to a wise and understanding officer, Captain R. H. Pratt, who did his best to give them training in handicrafts and in the white man's ways. In 1878 the government offered the imprisoned red men the choice of returning to the West or of receiving further education. The majority, most of them older men, chose to go home, but twenty-two of the younger Indians asked for further study. The opportunity to include a second colored race in his educational program intrigued General Armstrong, who agreed to accept fifteen as students at Hampton.

By no means all of the staff or friends of Hampton welcomed this innovation. Some feared that it would have an adverse effect on the Negro's development. Friends of the Indian, on the other hand, were alarmed lest the redmen be degraded. Some were afraid of hostility between the two races, while others warned against intermarriage and its complications. These dire predictions failed to move General Armstrong, who confidently insisted that the experiment would give "fresh life and force to the school."

The principal proved to be the better prophet. His students welcomed the Indians and tried to help them adjust to the life of the school. The Indians, while they gave up their traditional habit of smoking with great reluctance — Hampton rigidly enforced a "No Smoking" rule — did their best to reciprocate. When only a few weeks had demonstrated that most of the fears about the experiment were groundless, General Armstrong determined to expand the program. After hastily constructing a dormitory, which was promptly dubbed the "Wigwam," the principal accepted forty-nine more Indian youths recruited in the West. He then invited Booker Washington to undertake the assignment of living in the "Wigwam" with the sixty-odd Indian boys, handling discipline, teaching them to care for themselves and their quarters, and acting generally as a sort of "housefather" to them.

Washington took advantage of the opportunity not only to teach his Indian charges but to learn from them. He found that the Indian students mastered both academic studies and trades as well as the Negroes and that they reacted to kindness or ill treatment in essentially the same way as other human beings. His principal difficulty came with the attempt to "civilize" the Indian students, who parted with their pipes, braids, and blankets only with great reluctance. In the matter of shoes, however, it was the Indians who did the converting. Their moccasins were manifestly so comfortable that the entire campus soon gave up shoes for Indian footwear.

While acting as housefather to the Indian boys, Washington had an experience which impressed upon him the absence of logic in traditional Southern attitudes toward race. When one of his charges became ill, Washington was commissioned to deliver the boy to the Secretary of the Interior in the nation's capital. The two of them made the trip by steamer. When the bell rang for dinner, Washington circumspectly waited until most of the passengers had finished their meal before taking the Indian boy into the dining saloon. Politely the young Negro was informed that only the Indian could be served. Virtually the same experience was repeated on their arrival when the clerk of the hotel to which they had been directed would admit the Indian but refused to accommodate his teacher.

After a year the Indian experiment was so obviously successful that no one questioned it, and until 1912, when government aid for the project was discontinued, Indians regularly attended the Institute. The soundness of the idea having been proved at Hampton, the government established the Indian School at Carlisle Barracks, Pennsylvania, to provide training for Indians on a much larger scale.

Having demonstrated his skill in handling the Indian students, Washington shouldered the burden of another experiment at the beginning of his second year on the Hampton staff. General Armstrong had long been troubled by the earnest desire for education on the part of many Negroes who had no means of meeting even a small part of their expenses. In case after case it was the same: a willingness to do anything to earn the necessary money, but a shortage of self-help jobs. Selecting a few of the most promising applicants, he offered them work in one of the Institute's industries during the daytime and academic training at night. The money they earned would pay their current expenses and a little more; the surplus would be credited to their account in the Hampton treasury. When, after a year or two, they had built up enough credit, they would be transferred to the day school.

Washington took on the new work with enthusiasm. His twelve students, whom he saw only during the evening, worked for ten hours before reporting to him, the men in the sawmill and the women in the laundry. Applying a bit of practical psychology, he dubbed his group "The Plucky Class," giving each a certificate attesting to his "good and regular standing." Within a period of weeks the class had grown to twenty-five, and after many of its members had successfully made the transition to the regular classes of the Institute, the night school was incorporated as a regular and growing feature. As such it was only one of the many Hampton ideas which Washington was to take with him to Tuskegee.

I V

Tuskegee: The Experiment

ONE EVENING at the end of Washington's second year on the staff at Hampton, General Armstrong read in chapel the letter from Alabama requesting a teacher for a Negro school. The next morning the General asked his young protégé if he could handle the assignment. Washington thought he could, and the principal wrote back recommending him to the Tuskegee commissioners. Several days passed. Then came the telegram accepting the suggestion.

The words "Booker T. Washington will suit us" were a tonic to the entire Hampton community. Washington was a home-grown product, typical of the Institute's best. For the white teachers his new assignment confirmed their faith that the freedman, given the opportunity, could develop into the equal of the white man. To the Negro students the event meant more: never before had such a responsibility been given to one of their number. Hampton operated on the principle, which they accepted, that the Negro must look to the white man for training. But here was a former slave elevated to the leadership level formerly reserved for whites. He was each of them, raised to the highest potential. Proudly they sent him on his way, knowing intuitively that men like him carried the future of the race on their shoulders.

Before making the long trip south, Washington went back once more to Malden. Not improbably the strongest drawing card was the presence of Fannie Smith, a girl whom he had known since childhood and with whom he had kept in touch during his years at Hampton. One of the pupils in his school whom he had trained for further study, she was to graduate from Hampton in 1882.

Until he went to Tuskegee, Washington's range of experience had been narrow indeed. Except for his early existence on the plantation, of which he had only scattered recollections, he had called Malden "home" all his twenty-five years. He had spent a total of five years at Hampton. Only his study at Wayland Seminary, the summer at Saratoga, and the short venture into law had taken him out of the Malden-Hampton orbit.

His contacts had also been limited. Other than the strong formative influence of his mother in his early years, the forces which had done most to shape his character, intellect, and ideals had flowed mainly from New England. Mrs. Ruffner had first set for him tangible standards above those of the environment into which he had been born; the New England "missionaries" of Hampton like Mary Mackie and Nathalie Lord had kept him moving in the same direction. Above all he had been influenced by General Armstrong, educated at Williams College as a protégé of Mark Hopkins. All these persons had in common high integrity, a robust individualism, a strictly conventional outlook on moral problems, a strong humanitarianism, and a deep loyalty to the Protestant ethic of selflessness and service.

With such a background Washington went to Tuskegee to duplicate as nearly as possible what he had known at Hampton. Almost every important feature later found at Tuskegee could be traced back to its counterpart at the mother institution, and most of Washington's ideas and methods could be traced back to Armstrong. Mary Mackie, who visited Tuskegee in 1884 when it was only three years old, wrote that "the dial of time must have been turned back twelve years in its course" — that the little school in the Alabama Black Belt was exactly like the Hampton she had known when she first arrived in Virginia from New England.

Washington took with him to Tuskegee not only educational methods but basic assumptions about the Negro race in America. An intimate knowledge of his own people had convinced him, first, that emancipation had not brought the millennium and, second, that the freedman could not hope to step immediately into a position of equality with his favored white neighbors. He recognized that the Negro was inferior — not innately so, but in the cultural, social, and economic heritage necessary to compete on favorable terms in a white man's world.

The problem, to his mind, called for a long-range solution. Accepting the popular judgment of the early 1880's, he agreed that Reconstruction had been a serious mistake: "In a word, too much stress was placed upon the mere matter of voting and holding political office rather than upon the preparation for the highest citizenship." That the Negro's head had been turned by the glitter of political office and preferment was only natural, but the reaction which had stripped from the Negro all the badges of political recognition proved the folly of his brief excursion into politics.

Washington was convinced that the Negro must prove himself, must demonstrate tangibly and concretely that he was worthy of the blessings of liberty. He must destroy the stereotype which years of slavery had fixed in the minds of even his friends and eliminate each of the negative slave characteristics which still clung to him. He must substitute efficiency for the slipshod work of slavery days, responsibility for irresponsibility, knowledge for ignorance and superstition, accepted moral standards for the amorality of the slave quarters. The blame for the Negro's shortcomings was academic; the shortcomings were real and had to be remedied.

To accomplish this task required inculcation of a new set of values in keeping with accepted American tradition. Such an education could not be acquired through traditional methods; the Negro needed much more than academic training. Despite the good intentions of the New England missionaries who had come South after the war, they had made the mistake of assuming that what was applicable in one situation was necessarily applicable in another; consequently, they had tried to give the untrained black man the same education given in New England to white children with centuries of tradition behind them. As a result, "We had scores of young men learned in Greek, but few in carpentry or mechanical drawing. We had trained many in Latin, but almost none as engineers, bridge-builders, and machinists. Numbers were taken from the farm and educated, but were educated in everything else except agriculture."

Washington, following the Hampton model, proposed to

take the young men and young women from the farm, educate them in agriculture, and send them back as the backbone of a solid and prosperous citizenry. After the Negro had acquired a reputation as a property owner and a productive member of the community, would come the time for purely "cultural" training. Had the Pilgrim fathers and their immediate posterity not undergone a long tutelage to the soil? The Negro had to go through a similar process; for the present he must concern himself not with learning how to enjoy life, but with how to make a living. In industry, Washington insisted, the foundation for the future must be laid. From such a foundation would grow "habits of thrift, a love of work, economy, ownership of property, bank accounts." These in turn would produce "moral and religious strength" and the wealth "from which alone can come leisure and the opportunity for the enjoyment of literature and the fine arts."

Here was the basic justification for the "industrial education" gospel which Washington preached for the next thirty-five years. Primarily, it was education of a strictly utilitarian nature designed to prepare the student for a gainful occupation in agriculture or trade. Only by learning modern methods could the Negro hope to integrate himself successfully into the economy of his region. If he chose to be a farmer, as did the majority of Southern Negroes, he could not continue to cut oats with a hand scythe while the white farmer drove a harvester. "Let us give the black man so much skill and brains," said Washington, "that he can cut oats like the white man; then he can compete with him." If he chose a trade, the Negro must learn to produce what the community needed. In the postwar

South brickmaking, carpentry, and wagon making were far more important to the Negro than the classics.

Washington did not, however, ignore the value of the liberal arts. In the first place, his choice of industrial education for the Negro was essentially a matter of timing. "Perhaps all of us agree," he explained, "that that training is best which gives the student the broadest and most complete knowledge of the arts, sciences, and literature of all the civilized nations." But "where the want of time and money prevents this broader culture," he wished "to give the student that training in his own language, in the arts and sciences that will have special bearing on his life." Furthermore, Washington insisted that industrial education was not exclusive; that "thorough academic and religious training" must go "side by side" with industrial; that Tuskegee stood for an integrated training of the head, heart, and hand. Finally, he stubbornly battled the assumption that he advocated "class education" designed to fix the status of the Negro race as hewers of wood and drawers of water. Quite the opposite: industrial education would release the black man from drudgery by teaching him to make the forces of nature and modern science work for him.

Such ideas were completely foreign to both the white and Negro people of Macon County, Alabama, when Washington arrived there in June, 1881. Most white Southerners thought of the "educated Negro" in caricature, an affected, incongruously dressed dandy with spats, gloves, and cane. Education had done little, so far as they could observe, to improve the few Negroes exposed to it. It had made the Negro "uppity," had caused him to forget his "place," had implanted in him "high and mighty" ideas and aspirations. It had made him dissatisfied with his former occupation but had fitted him for nothing else. The white farmer in particular was sure that the best way to ruin a good Negro farm hand was to "educate" him.

The Southern Negro's conception of education differed only in his evaluation of its results. The educational process had the immense practical value, in his eyes, of raising its product to the status of the professional man and allowing him, as teacher, preacher, or politician, to live off the community. Education was desirable chiefly because it provided the only escape from manual labor; in addition it had the pleasing effect of setting the "educated" man apart as a superior being. The Negro boys who went away to school came home to "astonish the old folks with the new and strange things they had learned." If they "could speak a few words in some strange tongue," it made their parents proud and happy. Furthermore, the Negro teachers often yielded to the temptation "to keep everything connected with education in a sort of twilight realm of the mysterious and supernatural." Quite unconsciously "they created in the minds of their pupils the impression that a boy or girl who had passed through certain educational forms and ceremonies had been initiated into some sort of secret knowledge that was inaccessible to the rest of the world."

In the face of such notions, Washington saw that his first task at Tuskegee was to "sell" the idea of industrial education to both races. The whites were less difficult to persuade. Influential white citizens had been primarily responsible for bringing him to Tuskegee, and he shared many of their ideas about the Negro; he could show that the training he proposed to offer would solve many of the difficulties which the Negro's status as a freedman had raised. He was not afraid to let it be known that one of his objectives was indeed to "spoil" the Negro farm hand, to whom could be charged much of the waste and inefficiency of Southern agriculture. But Washington promised to replace him not with an educated dandy, but with a more responsible, skillful, law-abiding worker who would make a direct contribution to the welfare of the community.

Most of his early effort in public relations he spent on his own race in and around Tuskegee. He was eager not only to preach his gospel but to learn as much as possible about the conditions under which Negroes of Macon County lived. The conditions were anything but promising. Fewer than one hundred of the twenty-five thousand Negroes who lived within a radius of twenty miles of Tuskegee owned any land at all; the rest were sharecroppers or tenants who mortgaged the yield of their few acres in return for subsistence. Like the man hugging a bear, they wanted desperately to free themselves from the system of "advances" which kept them always in debt to the neighborhood merchant, but could not afford to let go. Knowing little or nothing of proper fertilization or of crop rotation and diversification, they planted cotton, and nothing but cotton, from the outer reaches of their farms to the very doors of the cabins they called home.

Vassalage to King Cotton also blinded them to the possibilities of bettering their condition by raising their own food. In a country where pigs, chickens, ducks, geese, berries, peaches, plums, vegetables, nuts, and other foods could be produced with relatively little effort, Washington found even the best of the Negro population eating salt pork from Chicago and canned chicken and tomatoes from Omaha. Most did not fare that well, for the combined forces of poverty, ignorance, and habit kept them on the old slave diet of fatback, corn bread, black-eyed peas, and an occasional ration of molasses. Improper nutrition in turn contributed to a high incidence of disease and early mortality.

Nor had housing improved greatly since slavery days. Former slave cabins served many as homes, while new houses largely followed the pattern of one-room dwellings not unlike the kitchen in which Booker Washington had spent the first nine years of his life. The furniture that graced these unpainted, weather-beaten cabins came as castoffs from white families or was crudely knocked together from scrap lumber. Sanitation facilities did not exist. When the new teacher, on his visits to these cabins, asked for a place to wash, his best hope was to find a single washbasin on a rack outside the house.

The lack of any real family life disturbed Washington even more. One-room living, hardly conducive to modesty, contributed to loose morality among the Negro population. Existence was geared to the needs of the cotton crop; the mother and children all wielded hoes and, when picking time came, went to the fields with gunny sacks over their shoulders. Babies, laid down at the ends of the rows, were cared for at intervals by their mothers or by one of the older children. As in slavery days, there were no organized meals at which the family sat down together.

Saturdays and Sundays provided the only break in an otherwise monotonous existence. Saturday meant a trip to town, when young and old piled into the family wagon and rumbled off to spend the day on the streets of Tuskegee. Essential purchases took only a few minutes, but the real enjoyment of the day came from window-shopping, gossiping with neighbors, and loafing about the stores and courthouse. Liquor, with resulting arguments and fights, contributed to the day's program for many. On Sunday they took picnic lunches to all-day church services which, with their shouting, singing, and emotional preaching, brought a welcome release from everyday problems.

For a month Washington made his way along the country roads of the county, introducing himself and begging a night's lodging at cabins along the way. This firsthand observation convinced him more than ever of the need for the type of training he hoped to inaugurate at Tuskegee, for the few Negroes who had had any education were doing little or nothing to improve their lot. "I found young men," he reported, "who could wrestle successfully with the toughest problems in 'compound interest or banking' or 'foreign exchange,' but who had never thought of trying to figure out why their fathers lost money on every bale of cotton raised." He found girls "who could locate on the map accurately the Alps and the Andes, but who had no idea of the proper position of the knives and forks on the dinner table."

Yearning to give these young people practical help in raising their standard of living, Washington recruited thirty students for his new school during his first tour of the countryside. This was not merely a sales effort, but a process of conscious selection. He well knew that any Negro school could have a large enrollment if it admitted aspirants of all ages and made no requirements as to previous training. He had taught such a school in Malden. But his ambition for the new institution was much higher. Remarkably able to concentrate on the task at hand without losing sight of long-range goals, he wanted it to be a lighthouse for Negro education in the deep South. In every one of the youths at Tuskegee he would attempt to instill the sense of mission so deeply rooted in his own being; he would make plain that every day at the school was a sacred day that belonged to the Negro race. Tuskegee existed, he would tell them, "that we may give you intelligence, skill of hand, and strength of mind and heart; and we help you in these ways that you, in turn, may help others."

In accordance with this purpose he accepted only students over sixteen who could already read and write. Such a limitation enabled him to choose his raw material. Scattered about through the county were a few teachers with at least a rudimentary education, and they in turn had passed on what they knew to a few young people despite the limited school sessions and the lack of a compulsory attendance law. From this group came most of the candidates who enrolled in the first class at Tuskegee Normal and Industrial Institute.

Despite some misunderstanding as to the nature of his project, Washington had the co-operation of both whites and Negroes. George W. Campbell and M. B. Swanson, the two white men on the board appointed by the Alabama Legislature, eased his path by giving the infant school their endorsement. Through Lewis Adams, the Negro member of the board, he obtained the loan of the A. M. E. Zion Church and the dilapidated shanty on its grounds. Shortly thereafter Campbell also contributed a blind horse, the first livestock owned by Tuskegee Institute.

Washington began by giving an entrance examination in arithmetic, grammar, and history, on the basis of which he classified his thirty students. They were somewhat startled, on the second day, to find their twenty-five-year-old teacher particular about matters which had no connection with schoolbooks. Lining the entire school up for the first of its regular daily inspections, he called attention to missing buttons, grease spots, dirty collars, and other failures to meet the standard of neatness and cleanliness he insisted upon. By doing so, he served notice that education at Tuskegee would concern itself with every area of the student's life, and that care of the body was to him as important as cultivation of the mind.

The church he continued to use as an assembly room for the school; the shanty, inadequate as it was, he divided into two sections in order to have some semblance of classes. As the early weeks went by, more students came, students whom Washington felt he could not turn away. He could not handle the task alone, and when the number reached fifty, he hired another teacher to share the load. Olivia A. Davidson, later to become his second wife, arrived at the end of August, when the school was only two months old. A part of Tuskegee Institute almost from its beginning, she helped to shape it in the early stages nearly as much as Washington himself did.

Olivia Davidson brought to Tuskegee qualities of zeal, persistence, and devotion to her race which matched Washington's in intensity. In addition she brought an abundance of native intelligence, tact, organizational ability, and a background which included broader training than his and a wealth of invaluable contacts in the East. Like Washington a Virginian by birth, she was two years older than he. As a child she had gone with her parents to Ohio, where she had had the advantage of public-school education. Feeling a strong obligation to serve her people, she went back South in the early seventies to teach in the rural districts of Mississippi. Here she remained for five years. She was teaching in Memphis when the great yellow fever epidemic of 1878 struck the city and immediately volunteered to become a nurse. When her services were refused because she was not strong enough, she decided to go to Hampton to prepare herself more adequately for teaching.

Her training and experience having advanced her far beyond most students entering Hampton, she went into the senior class and graduated with honors at the end of the year, in 1879. In all likelihood she listened with her classmates as the young West Virginia schoolteacher, fresh from his year at Wayland Seminary, delivered the commencement address on "The Force That Wins."

Through the generosity of Mrs. Augustus Hemenway of Boston, a friend who recognized her superior talents, she studied for the next two years at Framingham State Normal School in Massachusetts. At Framingham she deepened and broadened her knowledge, meanwhile winning the respect and affection of fellow students from some of the most respected families in the Boston area. Here she also demonstrated convincingly her integrity and loyalty to her race. Light-skinned enough to pass for white, she was told when she entered the Massachusetts school that she need not reveal herself as a Negro. She replied that she was not ashamed of her people, and that she wished to help make the term Negro as honorable as the name of any other race. Immediately after her graduation in August, 1881, she accepted the position offered her by Booker T. Washington as teacher and assistant principal at Tuskegee. During Washington's lifetime she was the only person given that title.

Olivia Davidson's arrival at Tuskegee was well timed. Taking over half the duties in the schoolroom shanty, she cheerfully disregarded the fact that crowded, miserably inadequate facilities and poorly prepared students made impossible a well-organized program. Washington had spent neither time nor money in repairing the building; perhaps, since he had no intention of remaining there, he did not think it worth the effort. The rain still poured in through the open windows and holes in the roof, often leaving not a dry spot in either of the two "classrooms." The start of a downpour was a signal for students to come forward and hold an umbrella over each of the teachers while they heard recitations. Living conditions for the two partners in the enterprise were not much better, for the house in which they boarded also leaked badly, and the landlady often had to perform a similar service while they ate their meals.

Because he knew the Institute could not long continue under such conditions, Washington had been trying hard to find a more suitable location. Other reasons made the move necessary. Since all the students boarded in the town of Tuskegee, few could muster enough money to support themselves through a nine months' term. Unless they could find some way to earn their board and room, the school would disintegrate. The obvious solution was a farm on which they could raise enough food to become at least partly self-sufficient. "We began with agriculture because we had to eat," Washington said.

A farm represented more than mere subsistence, however. Since 85 per cent of the Negro population of the gulf states made their living from the land, agriculture logically formed the backbone of the vocational training the Institute was to offer. The farm would enable Washington to develop the "industrial" side of the curriculum and to guarantee that his students "would be sure of knowing how to make a living after they had left us." A permanent location with living quarters for the students would also make possible the training in personal hygiene, thrift, and economy which the principal and his assistant considered so vital to their program.

Fortunately, Washington learned toward the end of the summer that an abandoned plantation about a mile from town could be bought for $500. There was a reason for the low price: the "big house" had burned and the entire plantation had been allowed to run down. Its four buildings — a small cabin, an old stable, a chicken house, and a prewar kitchen — were in no better condition than the shanty, but here was something to build on. The young principal's mouth watered.

Naturally he turned back to Hampton. Outlining the situation to General Marshall, the treasurer, he explained that the owner of the farm would accept a down payment of $250 and the remainder in twelve months. Could the Hampton treasury possibly advance its daughter institution the amount of the down payment? General Marshall replied that he had no authority to divert funds belonging to Hampton, but would gladly lend Washington $250 from his personal account.

The loan from General Marshall, gratefully accepted, was the first of many gambles prompted by Washington's determination, ambition, and thoroughgoing self-confidence. The responsibility for this initial plunge weighed heavily on him during the following months, for he had no idea where he would get the money to repay the general, much less the balance due on the plantation at the end of the year. It was his good fortune that in the early days, before he had developed his unrivaled skill at fund raising, he had Olivia Davidson to help him.

The purchase of the farm gave new impetus to the school's development, not only by encouraging the students but by offering tangible evidence of the two young teachers' resourcefulness and faith to both white and Negro people of the county. Recitations went on in the shanty during the mornings, while in the afternoons the students went to the farm to work. Within a few weeks the stable and henhouse became classrooms and the other two buildings stood ready for occupancy. Proud of their achievement, students and teachers moved the school to its new location.

Washington now had to face the problem of selling his students on the idea of industrial education. Their training had been exclusively academic, as most of them thought it should be, and he was apprehensive about their reaction to the hard work involved in clearing the farm and planting crops. One morning shortly after the move to the plantation he announced that the next day they would dismiss school early and hold a "chopping bee." All who had axes or could borrow them were to bring them along; he would try to supply the others. The next morning, as one of the students described it, they were all "excited and eager for that chopping bee" and "were all discussing what it would be like, because we had never been to one before." When school was over, Washington shouldered his ax and led the way to the woods, where his charges soon learned that "a chopping bee, as he called it, was no different from just plain cutting down trees and clearing the land. There wasn't anything new about that — we all had had all we wanted of it." Only the fact that the principal worked harder, faster, and more skillfully than anyone else prevented an open rebellion.

Gradually Washington tried to break down the prejudice of his students against the industrial phase of his program, at first speaking to them "gently and even cautiously" about it. For the most part, sharing the prevailing conceptions of education, they confidently expected their study at the Institute to provide an escape from the kind of work they had known. In addition, those who had already had a taste of teaching felt that manual labor was beneath their dignity. The principal's desire that all should prepare themselves to go back to the rural districts from which they came antagonized others who hoped to leave the farm for the towns and cities. Perhaps the most serious argument was the universal contention that they had lived on farms all their lives and knew all about agriculture. The fact that the first year's "training" would necessarily consist of grubbing up stumps, felling trees, building fences, digging ditches, and plowing fields made the argument even more difficult to answer.

The parents of the students, having sent them off to school to advance them in the social and economic scale, shared the attitude of their sons and daughters, and for several years many new arrivals at Tuskegee bore painstakingly scrawled notes requesting that they be taught "book learning," but not be required to work. Far from acceding to these requests, Washington required that every student participate in the industrial as well as in the academic phase of the curriculum. Either was useless, he felt, without the other.

Washington also had to meet the argument, chiefly among the older people, that the new Institute was "God-less" and "un-Christian." He was orthodox enough in his beliefs and an open advocate of religious activity; he had been a member of the Baptist Church since childhood and had "learned to love" the Bible at Hampton. But theology did not interest him, and he had little patience with the "narrow denominational spirit" which burned in many church members. Characteristically, he was interested in the practical value of religion as applied to everyday liv-ing; as he told his students at Tuskegee, "the religion of Christ is a real and helpful thing that you can take with you into your classrooms, into your shops, onto the farm."

The fact that he created an atmosphere at the Institute which was nonsectarian, though deeply religious, fur-nished one of the principal bases for the charge that the school was "Godless." Since it had no connection with an organized church, many Negroes assumed that its reli-gious fervor must be low indeed. Furthermore, Washing-ton did not conceal his lack of respect for the Negro min-istry and deplored the clergy's low standards of education and ethics. Many of them, in his opinion, were worthless, idle men unable or unwilling to make an honest living with their hands. An enthusiastic believer in the public-school system, he could not forgive the misplaced zeal which set up struggling little denominational schools in competition with public institutions, crippling the latter and robbing "innocent children" of an adequate elemen-tary education. But most of all he condemned the preach-ers' failure to make religion meaningful and useful; they should not, he insisted, feed the people "old, worn-out theological dogmas," but should give them "inspiration and direction in practical work of community building, connecting religion with every practical and progressive movement for the improvement of the home and community life."

During the early months of the school's existence he spent every week end away from Tuskegee, continuing his campaign to make the Institute better known, break down prejudice against it, and recruit more students. Having no horse nor wagon, he made it a point each week to enlist the help of some colored citizen who did. As one of his staff put it, "When he needed anything, he'd go out and put his hand on it"; stopping "some old black man" in the street, he would say, "Now, Uncle, you can help by bringing your wagon and mule round at nine o'clock Saturday morning for me to go off round the country telling the people about the school." "Uncle" would be there, and Washington's transportation was assured for another week end.

Meanwhile, Olivia took the major responsibility for raising money to pay for the farm. She organized "festivals," or bazaars, to which countless families, white and black, contributed cakes, pies, and other home products, and made house-to-house canvasses for direct contributions. Well-wishers of both races, urged to make the school their own by having a part in the purchase of the farm, sent or brought their offerings. Contributions ranged from five cents up; many of the gifts came in the form of produce the school could use. One seventy-year-old woman hobbled up to Washington with the words, "Mr. Washin'ton, God knows I spent de bes' days of my life in slavery. God knows I's ignorant an' poor, but I knows what you an' Miss Davidson is tryin' to do. I ain't got no money, but I wants you to take dese six eggs, what I's been savin' up, an' put dese six eggs into de eddication of dese boys an' gals."

Within three months Washington was able to repay the $250 to General Marshall; two months later he paid the remaining $250 and received the deed to the property. Meanwhile, despite the opposition of the Negro clergy, he made rapid headway in his effort to make the school "a real part of the community in which it was located." The Negroes increasingly appreciated his efforts; if his charm, eloquence, and persuasive arguments had not converted them, a natural pride in a flourishing enterprise directed by one of their own race would have done so.

The whites, too, looked on with an approval which many of them expressed in the tangible form of contributions. Washington won their confidence by his own circumspect behavior and his emphasis on thrift, industry, and responsibility — teaching which they correctly judged would exert a salutary influence on the Negro from the white man's point of view. But they saw also that as it progressed, the school would bring an increased flow of trade to Tuskegee and that local merchants would benefit from a rising level of prosperity among the Negroes of the county. Aside from self-interest, many white citizens unquestionably had a genuine, if paternalistic, interest in the colored half of the population and took real pride in the fact that their town was helping to support an institution for the education of the former slaves.

Astute as he was, Washington lost no opportunity to praise both white and black citizens of Tuskegee, but especially the white, for their liberality and interest. "Tuskegee is inhabited by some of the most cultured and liberal white people to be found in any portion of the South," he often said. Partly such statements stemmed from sincere gratitude, but partly they were a conscious attempt to enlist co-operation by an appeal to the better side of human nature. His strategy was to gain more for his cause by praising the virtues of the white South than by condemning its faults.

His remarkable success in transforming the school from an "experiment" into "an established fact" during the next fifteen years justified this strategy. On one occasion he said that to read the history of Tuskegee Institute would be to read his biography. Until 1895, as he threw his great creative energies into the single task of undergirding and shaping the institution he had founded, the statement was largely true.

V

Tuskegee: Established Fact

THE EARLY YEARS of Tuskegee Institute saw Grover Cleveland become the first Democratic President since the Civil War, lose to Benjamin Harrison four years later, and move triumphantly back to the White House in 1893. As men like Vanderbilt and Gould inaugurated the era of the multimillionaire industrialist, the American Federation of Labor emerged from the seething strikes of the eighties and nineties as the dominant force in the labor movement. Thousands of penniless immigrants overflowed the eastern ports, creating a new issue in American politics, while the demand of embattled farmers for agrarian reform and cheap money culminated in the Populist wave of 1892 and the free-silver campaign of 1896. The entire nation, during those two decades, felt the growing pains of a new industrial society.

To Booker T. Washington the principal difficulty of the era was finding the money to keep Tuskegee going. The appropriation from the legislature did not cover even instructional salaries, and the continuing increase in students, since few could pay their own way, meant little additional revenue. Furthermore, though the people of Tuskegee had helped as generously as they could, the future demanded larger gifts than cakes and pies to sell at bazaars.

Washington turned for funds toward the industrial North and East. In this effort Olivia Davidson contributed more than moral support, for it was she who made the first trips to New England in search of financial support. Sometimes too tired at night to undress, she often drove herself beyond the limits of her endurance. At one home she was admitted by the maid and asked to wait in the living room; a few minutes later the lady on whom she was calling arrived to find her asleep from exhaustion.

On many occasions while Olivia was in the East, Washington waited anxiously for money with which to meet their obligations. At one such time not a penny was in the treasury to repay a $400 debt; the morning the note fell due, a check for the exact amount arrived from Olivia. One of the old employees of Tuskegee recalled that he used to take the wheelbarrow each morning and go to the office where Washington opened the mail. "If there was money in the mail, then I could go along to the town with the wheelbarrow and get provisions, and if there was no money, then there was no occasion to go to town, and we'd just eat what we had left."

The principal burden of fund raising, however, fell on Washington. Olivia helped him not only by providing an entree to influential people, but by working with him on his speeches to improve their effectiveness. Other friends also aided in launching that part of his career at which he was to become a past master. Before he went North the first time in 1882, General Armstrong advised him what to say and how to say it. "Give them an idea for every word," he told his young protégé. General Armstrong also furnished him, then and later, with fulsome letters of recommendation endorsing Tuskegee and stating that as much as any man in the land Washington was "securing to the whole country the moral results which the Civil War meant to produce." Washington also carried letters from the county and state superintendents of education and an endorsement from the governor.

Despite such encouragement he found money raising "hard, disagreeable, wearing work." On his first trip, anything but sure of himself, he sought advice in New York from one of the secretaries of an organization deeply interested in the Negro, only to be told that he would be lucky to raise his travel expenses. As Washington frankly admitted later, "This tended to take the heart out of me," but he could not turn back without having made an effort.

Going on to Massachusetts, he made his first address in the little town of Chicopee, near Springfield, at the morning service of the Congregational Church. The fact that several of his hearers spoke favorably afterwards encouraged him, but since he had only one speech, which he had memorized word for word, he was embarrassed to learn that they planned to be present when he spoke at a nearby town that evening. The pessimistic warning he had received earlier was well-founded. The fact that some Negroes had exploited New England humanitarian sympathies by soliciting funds for nonexistent causes made it difficult for him to get an audience. Many prominent persons, beleaguered by representatives of various organizations, refused to see him. Early in May, 1882, after he had collected a total of only $53 in two days of pavement pounding, he wrote in the fragmentary diary he kept during the trip that things looked "rather gloomy."

Still, he was treated kindly in most instances, and the letter from General Armstrong, who was well-known in New England, often opened the door to him. In churches and town halls, before various kinds of organizations and charitable groups, wherever he could get an audience, he told the story of Tuskegee. Mainly, of course, the Institute needed money, but he and Olivia always appealed for books and clothing as well. As the amount of money raised on these trips gradually increased, the early trickle of other gifts also became a steady stream which flowed southward for years. Even after Tuskegee had grown to considerable proportions, Washington took a particular pleasure in these donations. He would have the boxes and barrels opened in his office and would turn aside from far more urgent business to sort out the offerings and decide which boy or girl, or which family, could best use them.

During the summer of 1882, after his first excursion into the North, Washington went back to Malden to marry Fannie N. Smith. He was twenty-six at the time; she was twenty-four, and had graduated from Hampton shortly before their wedding. Her coming to Tuskegee enabled Washington to offer a home to his teachers, who moved in with him and his bride after they set up housekeeping. More than this, Mrs. Washington filled a void in the curriculum by offering in her home the rudiments of what later became home-economics courses for the girls.

Fannie Smith Washington died in May, 1884, less than a year after the birth of a daughter to whom she and her husband gave the name Portia. Whatever his reason, Washington in his autobiographical writings of later years said little of his first wife. She was remembered in Tuskegee as a kind, modest person, eager and willing to serve both the school and the community.

During the first two years, by their combined efforts, Washington and his assistant principal raised more than $11,000; in the third year alone the figure reached $10,-000. Much of this came in relatively small contributions, with Negroes continuing to bring in offerings of produce or stock whenever they had a few chickens or a hog to spare. By far the largest part of the cash donations went into buildings, for Washington confessed that he rarely had the funds to pay for a new structure at the time he authorized its construction: "The large increase in the number of students tempted us often to put up buildings for which we had no money. In the early days of the institution by far the larger proportion of the buildings were begun on faith." The proportion of cash to faith in one instance was only $200 out of a total cost of $8000.

At first, tangible evidence of progress on the old Varner plantation was slow, for keeping the school together, putting the farm and its four small buildings in condition for use, and planting the first year's crops demanded all the energies of students and teachers alike. But during the second year Tuskegee citizens who rode out in their buggies for a look at the Negro school could see that a substantial building was well under way. The three-story frame structure, almost square and boxlike in appearance, was dedicated at the second-anniversary celebration in 1883. The first floor provided classroom space; the second, a small chapel for devotions and public exercises; and the third, dormitory space for the girls. Washington named the building Porter Hall in honor of A. H. Porter of

Brooklyn, whose $500 donation was the largest received up to that time.

After completion of the building (one of the few at Tuskegee not constructed by student labor) the students dug out the basement in order to make space for a dining room, kitchen, and laundry. Though considerably better than they had had before, the new facilities were crude at best; in the basement dining room long tables with oil-cloth covers were set with the cheapest crockery and iron knives, forks, and spoons. The men students, still not provided for, had to be "scattered around in whatever places we could secure." The winter of 1882-1883 must have recalled to Washington the winter he spent in tents at Hampton, for like General Armstrong he made the rounds on cold nights to huts and shanties where he found his charges huddled together in front of open fires trying to keep warm. Deeply concerned for the welfare of his students, he winced when he overheard a girl exclaim in disgust that the rope at the well was broken and that a student "can't even get a drink of water at this school." Fortunately, most of the students were grateful for the opportunity to go to school under any circumstances.

The next few years saw a steady rise in material prosperity. In 1883 came the first gifts from the Slater and Peabody funds, both established to aid Southern education. With the money from the Slater Fund, Washington built a carpenter shop, set up a windmill to pump water to the school buildings, bought a sewing machine for the girl students, bought mules and wagons, and paid the farm manager's salary for nine months. During the same year the legislature, on recommendation of the Superintendent of Education, increased the annual appropriation for Tuskegee from $2000 to $3000. The bill passed after an eloquent appeal by Colonel W. F. Foster, the ex-Confederate soldier who had urged the initial appropriation for Tuskegee and who was then Speaker of the House of Representatives. With the exception of one year in which Washington got into "a very tight place" financially and had to borrow from General Armstrong, his trips North brought in more and more money; during the fifth year the contributions amounted to more than $20,000, a figure which continued to rise annually.

Increased resources and Washington's insistence that the institution, as it grew, should be built by the students themselves, stimulated the development of the industrial-training program. Recognizing that student workmanship would be inferior at first, he nevertheless felt that training in the construction trades and in self-reliance would outweigh the advantages of somewhat better buildings.

Just as they began with agriculture because they had to eat, Washington and his staff developed the trades at Tuskegee along natural lines as the need arose. The first building, Porter Hall, was not yet complete when the principal made plans for a larger brick structure, Alabama Hall. Discovering that the Institute's farm had deposits of very good clay, Washington determined to add brickmaking to the industrial program. There was another good reason: just as the school needed bricks, so did the town of Tuskegee, and Washington believed that the surest step to advancement for the Negro was to produce something which answered a real need of the community.

At the time, Washington knew absolutely nothing about

the brick industry. Assembling what literature he could find on the subject, he put his students to digging. The new venture proved little more popular than the "chopping bee," for the work was hard and dirty, and only after several trials did they find satisfactory clay. With the meager resources on hand Washington built a kiln and hopefully tried to fire the twenty-five thousand bricks his students had molded. Something — he did not know what — went wrong; apparently the kiln was improperly constructed. When, after more labor, a second kiln failed, most of the students gave up. Enlisting the aid of several of the teachers, Washington began again. His hopes rose as the burning of the third kiln (which required about a week) seemed on the point of success. Suddenly toward the end of the week the kiln fell.

Whether out of sheer stubbornness or out of an intuitive conviction that the job could be done, Washington refused to heed the arguments of his staff that brickmaking at Tuskegee was a failure. By that time, having no money with which to continue the experiment, he made a hurried trip to Montgomery and pawned his watch for fifteen dollars. With this new capital he began on the fourth kiln; this time, at the end of the week, he had bricks.

The time limit on his pawn ticket expired before he was able to redeem his watch, but as he wrote later, "I never regretted the loss of it." The brickmaking industry became Tuskegee's most valuable advertisement as white citizens who had had no interest in the school came to buy bricks. Seeing for themselves what Washington was doing, they spread the word in their own communities. As he said, the making of bricks caused many white residents "to begin to feel that the education of the Negro was not making him worthless," but was adding something to the wealth and comfort of the community. Brickmaking helped to lay the foundation for the pleasant relations which continued to exist between the Institute and the white people of the surrounding region.

The experiment in brickmaking took place in 1883. Carpentry, the other basic industry necessary to student construction of buildings, was made possible by the Slater Fund gift of the same year. With an eye not only to supplying a community need but to advertising, Washington added printing in 1885; this enabled him to publish a news bulletin called the *Southern Letter* which went out monthly to Tuskegee's widening circle of friends. The need for furnishing the dormitories prompted the addition of cabinet and mattress making in 1887. A year later came wheelwrighting and wagon building, and in 1889 Washington persuaded Lewis Adams to move his well-established shop to the Institute in order to provide training in shoemaking, harness making, and metal work.

In 1885, a year after the death of his first wife, Washington married Olivia Davidson. As they had for four years, they continued to pool their common energies in the work of the school. Keeping physical facilities and finances ahead of an ever-expanding enrollment absorbed a large share of their time and effort, but Washington and his assistant principal never lost their initial interest in the human raw material for which the school existed. The students considered Olivia Washington an "aristocrat," but the term carried no opprobrium whatever; a girl who entered with the original thirty in 1881 remembered her as "one of the noblest women who ever lived." She became a mother to the women students, most of whom had never been separated from their families before going to Tuskegee, and, in her own quiet way, something of a matchmaker. "She would point out a certain boy who had the qualities she found admirable," one of her students wrote. "He soon found himself the center of a group of girls." Her judgment and tact almost always enabled her to devise a solution for disciplinary problems.

Realizing that he had to go slow at first, Washington on his part worked constantly to instill the personal habits and traits of character which had been drilled into him at Hampton. When mere precept failed, he sought for ways to dramatize the lesson he was trying to put across. For example, after ineffective efforts to teach the students to put away their tools at night, he caused a mild sensation at "evening prayers" by interrupting the service to send three students back to the field for their implements. He explained to the group that "they would be more benefited by prayer and song after having done their work well than by leaving it poorly done."

His students thought the "gospel of the toothbrush" a mania with him. The conscious exaggeration of the importance of this symbol and the requirement that no student could remain at Tuskegee without it became so widely known among the Negro population that students who possessed nothing more than the clothes on their backs occasionally arrived with toothbrush in hand. Often they had had no occasion to use one before. On one tour of inspection the principal came to a room occupied by three girls who had just entered. Asked if they had toothbrushes, one of them replied, "Yes, sir. That is our brush. We bought it together, yesterday."

Along with the toothbrush went emphasis on the clean collar, the use of the nightgown, polished shoes, and of course the daily bath. "I want to see you own a decent home," Washington told his students. "And let me say right here that your home is not decent or complete unless it contains a good comfortable bathtub. Of the two, I believe I would rather see you own a bathtub without a house, than a house without a bathtub." Staff members stood by to scrutinize the appearance of the students as they marched in for each meal and for evening prayers, taking out of the line for correction any who failed to meet the standard. A boy or girl who was late to the dining room without good excuse went without the meal.

To Negro youths out of the Alabama cotton fields, life at Tuskegee was Spartan indeed. Not only did they have to meet strict requirements in regard to personal cleanliness; they were forbidden to use any form of alcoholic beverages or tobacco, nor could they play cards or dice. The days moved along with military precision, each hour accounted for down to five-minute intervals, from the five o'clock rising bell until the retiring bell at nine-thirty that evening. Until the mattress- and cabinet-making shop began to produce in relatively large quantities, they used barrels and boxes "in the raw state" for furniture and slept on crude frame bedsteads covered with straw-filled ticks. Though the Tuskegee chapel later boasted the first electric light in Macon County, during the early years students read by the light of large lamps suspended from the ceiling.

The Sunday schedule and the wealth of organized religious activity proved that Tuskegee was "nondenominational, but by no means nonreligious." The Sunday round of services included Christian Endeavor at nine, chapel at eleven, and Sunday School at one, with an enforced quiet hour from three to four. Only the band concert later in the afternoon allowed a secular note to creep in. In addition, students were required to attend daily chapel each evening from Monday through Thursday and prayer meeting on Friday night. The more devout also worshiped at a voluntary morning devotional just after breakfast each day and worked in the campus YMCA or YWCA organizations.

The most significant service of the week was the assembly on Sunday evening, when the principal gave his weekly talk — a practice modeled directly on General Armstrong's "Sunday-evening talks" at Hampton. In these conversational little homilies, many of which were later collected and published, Washington tried "to speak straight to the hearts of our students and teachers and visitors concerning the problems and questions that confront them in their daily life here in the South." The beginning of "Two Sides of Life" is typical: "There are quite a number of divisions into which life can be divided, but for the purposes of this evening I am going to speak of two: the bright side of life and the dark side." Other titles included "Helping Others," "The Virtue of Simplicity," "Have You Done Your Best?" "What Will Pay?" "The Importance of Being Reliable," "Keeping Your Word," "A Penny Saved," "The Gospel of Service" — a mixture of the New Testament, *Poor Richard's Almanack,* and the "self-help" doctrine popularized in that era by Samuel Smiles.

These talks, which gave a direct insight into Washington's personal philosophy, were platitudinous at best. But to his unsophisticated audience the principal was inspiration personified. As time went on, each talk was printed in the weekly newspaper, the *Student,* which was mailed to all Tuskegee graduates. A youth who entered as late as 1912 testified that the first "Sunday-evening talk" he heard, "Have a Place to Put Everything, and Put Everything in That Place," well-nigh revolutionized his life.

In the academic program at Tuskegee, Washington directed that every lesson have a direct application to the familiar in order to make it readily intelligible and meaningful to the student. An experience during his teaching at Malden had taught him the value of relating ideas to tangible realities. At recess period one day, after unsuccessfully trying to interest his pupils in a "dull, dry, stupid geography lesson," he joined them as they "scampered off" to wade in a nearby stream. Seeing the possibilities in the situation, Washington began to point out islands, capes, peninsulas, and lakes. His students immediately followed his example, and geography took on a new meaning.

Welding theory and practice, as he described it, meant specifically an infusion into such courses as mathematics and English composition subject matter related to the vocational training the students were then pursuing. In mathematics, a student of carpentry would be asked to determine which common length of board would suffice for a given job with a minimum of waste; a girl learning dressmaking, the smallest number of yards of cloth for making dresses of several sizes; a boy in agriculture, the selling price of his bales of cotton at the prevailing price per pound. For a class in spelling, the teacher would bring a small chest of drawers and the tools required to build it;

he would then ask the students to write correctly the name of each tool and part of the chest, together with related words which these brought to mind. "An ounce of application," Washington would say, "is worth a ton of abstraction."

As he expanded the physical facilities of Tuskegee, Washington also tried to build a staff sympathetic to his educational philosophy. Quite naturally he looked at first to Hampton for teachers. In the early years he relied mainly on Warren Logan, treasurer of the Institute, and on his brother John Washington, who directed the entire vocational-training program as Superintendent of Industries. These two, together with James N. Calloway, manager of the Institute's farm, constituted the first Finance Committee. Before the turn of the century the inner circle also included George Washington Carver, director of the agricultural-training program, and Emmett Scott, Washington's private secretary.

Logan went to Tuskegee in 1883 after thorough schooling in bookkeeping by General Marshall, treasurer of Hampton. Employed as a teacher, he soon demonstrated such ability that Washington made him treasurer of the Institute. He continued to teach several classes, however, and led the choir as well. Cheerful by disposition, he taught students the value of the dollar by forcing them to practice the most rigid economy and made them respect and like him for it. As acting principal during Washington's frequent absences from Tuskegee, Logan had a significant part in the everyday management of the institution.

John Washington arrived in 1885, the year Olivia Davidson and his brother Booker were married. He was one of those men who give character to an educational institution. Placed in charge of industrial training, he had the task of assigning each student to his work for the day. This, plus his duties as Commandant of Cadets (he enjoyed being called "Colonel") gave him avenues of contact with students which he welcomed. He encouraged the organization of a band at Tuskegee and took great interest in the baseball team. Though often stern and positive, he endeared himself to the students by his appreciation for and encouragement of the smallest degree of ability.

John Washington also possessed some of his brother's persistence and determination. On one occasion Alabama Polytechnic Institute offered him a large piece of machinery which he coveted for use in his industrial program. When Booker and Logan vetoed acceptance of the gift because of the tremendous shipping expense, John took a pair of oxen and dragged it over thirty miles of country roads to Tuskegee. In letters beginning, "My Dear Brother," John kept Booker informed during the latter's frequent absences from the school. A typical letter reports that students are continuing to come in every day, and that he needs about seventy-five more blankets; that he has written to the nursery for trees; that rain has interfered with the brickmaking. Which shall he plan to build first, he asks, the new laundry or the industrial building?

By 1888 the Institute had grown to such proportions that Washington decided to make the annual anniversary celebration an even more significant occasion than usual. Since the chapel of Porter Hall was inadequate, a large wooden pavilion was built to accommodate the crowd. On the day of the exercises more than two thousand people, including almost the entire Negro population of the town of Tuskegee and a large proportion of the white, overflowed the grounds. Besides a number of cottages and other small buildings, four major structures now graced the old Varner plantation. Alabama Hall, into which the first bricks had gone, had been completed in 1884 as a girls' dormitory, releasing space in Porter Hall for recitation rooms, offices, and library. Armstrong Hall housed the printing office and some of the men students. The latest building, just completed, Washington had named Olivia Davidson Hall as a tribute to his wife.

Alert to any opportunity to impress the public, Washington had every department humming during the morning hours. At the blacksmith and wheelwright shop the visitors could see wagons, small tools, spring-wagon seats, and other articles; in the carpenter shop, wardrobes, tables, wash stands, book cases, bedsteads, and chairs; in the printing office, checks, notes, catalogues, convention minutes, annual reports, letterheads, and invitations; at the laundry, freshly ironed bedding, dresses, collars, cuffs, shirts, underwear, table linen, and towels; and in the sewing room, clothing for men, women, and children. One hundred and twenty thousand bricks stood ready for burning at the brickyard, and stacks of lumber attested to the activity of the sawmill. The farm and poultry yards were exhibiting vegetables, hogs, cattle, chickens, turkeys, guineas, geese, eggs, and honey; while the cooking class had prepared cakes, jellies, bread, yeast, meats, and a roast pig. As if this were not enough, Washington herded all comers into the big pavilion for a full-scale dinner before the exercises began in the early afternoon.

At that time, only seven years after the school's founding, more than four hundred students were attending the

Institute. The farm had grown from the original one hundred acres to five hundred forty, and the property of the school was valued at $80,000. Income from all sources amounted to almost $27,000 for the year, which "about covered the expenses."

The next year, 1889, brought a great loss to Washington and Tuskegee in the death of Olivia Washington. Two sons, Baker Taliaferro (later changed to Booker Taliaferro, Jr.) and E. Davidson Washington, had been born to them since their marriage in 1885. Shortly after the birth of the second child Olivia suffered severe strain and exposure when hastily removed from the house to escape a fire. She died shortly thereafter in Boston, where Washington had taken her for treatment.

The part she had played in the building of Tuskegee had made for a doubly close bond between Olivia Washington and her husband. He never failed, in any later reference to her, to give her full credit for her contribution, often repeating that she had been more responsible for Tuskegee's early success than any other individual. Never a man to discuss his personal life, Washington left little or no record of his feelings beyond the expression of loss recorded later in his autobiography. One or two letters written by Olivia, however, reveal something of their relationship. One of those, an intimate letter which begins, "My dear husband," and ends, "Goodbye, dearest," is full of personal details about the children. "Watermelons are plentiful and Portia is happy," it reads. "You ought to be home to see how cute and sweet Brother is. He runs all about and has grown some."

Washington was an affectionate husband and father, snatching as many hours as he could from a busy schedule for time with his family. "When father wanted to make a speech," his daughter Portia recalled, "he would walk up and down and deliver the speech to me and ask how I liked it. I thought it was grand." During the years when his two sons were small he often took one or the other of them up on his gray horse or in his buggy as he rode about the Tuskegee grounds. His interest in his family extended beyond his wife and children. He always returned from his trips north bearing gifts for John's children as well as his own, and for years he contributed to the living expenses of his sister Amanda and her husband in Malden. After Olivia's death he continued to write to her mother, who affectionately addressed letters to him as, "Dear Son."

As the early nineties passed, Tuskegee continued to prosper under his never-flagging leadership. By 1895 the enrollment had reached eight hundred, and two hundred more applicants had been turned away during the year. The staff now numbered fifty-five, and the school owned, in the clear, property worth more than $200,000. More important, one hundred sixty-five graduates of Tuskegee were in the field, most of them as teachers. In Alabama, Tennessee, Florida, Kansas, Louisiana, Mississippi, Virginia, the history of Tuskegee's founding was being repeated as its graduates founded schools of their own. The fact that for ten years no parent had asked that his child be relieved from manual labor made Washington feel that he had revolutionized public opinion in regard to industrial education. By 1895 Tuskegee could justify General Armstrong's description of it as "the best product of Negro enterprise of the century."

V I

"The Broad Question of the Races"

THE 1880's and 1890's marked not only the growth of Tuskegee Institute, but the maturing of Washington's ideas and his emergence as a national spokesman for the Negro in the area of race relations. His first trips to the North and East established him as a speaker of uncommon ability, and his reputation grew steadily, particularly in educational circles. As early as 1884 he addressed four thousand members of the National Education Association in Madison, Wisconsin, and by 1888 he had served three terms as president of the Alabama State Teachers' Association. In 1893 the *Outlook,* a popular magazine of the day, published his picture along with pictures of Eliot of Harvard, Dwight of Yale, and Potter of Princeton in a feature article on the nation's twenty-eight leading college presidents.

One event, however, overnight stamped Washington's name into the consciousness of thousands who had never heard it before. His address at the Cotton States and International Exposition in 1895, later dubbed the "Atlanta Compromise" by his critics, represented Washington's de-

parture from the relatively restricted field of Negro education for the broader aspects of Negro-white relationships.
It immediately widened his circle of influence to include
hosts of persons who cared little about the former but had
a vital interest in the difficult problem of race relations
which had risen from the ashes of the Civil War. Both
North and South were tired of the problem, but neither
could ignore it. Consequently, when a prominent Negro
came forward with a specific solution, he was assured a
nationwide hearing; when his solution seemed reasonable and practical, he was also assured a nationwide following.

Stabilization of his personal life after the loss of Olivia
helped prepare the way for Washington's growth as a national spokesman for the Negro. In 1889, while attending
the commencement exercises at Fisk University, he sat at
dinner opposite a dynamic twenty-four-year-old senior
named Margaret Murray. She had planned to accept a
teaching job in Texas, but as a result of her meeting with
Washington she soon found herself at Tuskegee Institute
as "Lady Principal."

Margaret Murray had early demonstrated the independence and ability which qualified her for such a position.
One of ten children of a poverty-stricken family in Macon,
Mississippi, she left her family when her father died and
at the age of seven went to live with a white Quaker
schoolteacher and his sister. An avid reader, she confessed
that she was "not always a good child," and sometimes hid
under the house in order to study. When she was four-
teen, her benefactor asked, "Margaret, would thee like to
teach?" Borrowing a long skirt, she went to the office of a
local magistrate and presented herself for examination;

the next day she became a teacher in the school where she had formerly been a pupil. Later, in search of further training, she went to Fisk, where as a "half-rater," she worked her way through.

At Tuskegee her sympathy and understanding soon made her a "Mother Confessor" to both students and teachers. She also made a conquest of the principal. By 1891 she and Washington were informally engaged, and two years later they were married.

She was much troubled by the question of Washington's three children, the oldest of whom was then only seven. She did not particularly like "little folks" and felt especially ill at ease about Portia. "I somehow dread being thrown with her for a lifetime," she confessed in a letter written late in 1891. "I wonder, Mr. Washington, if it is a wise and Christian thing for me to love you feeling as I do." She was not, however, uninterested in the welfare of the children, who had been "farmed out" with various persons after Olivia Washington's death. In 1892 she wrote Washington that they were not being properly supervised, since Mrs. John Washington, who had them at the time, "knows as much as a cat about caring for children." Despite the difficulties of the situation both Margaret and the children made a satisfactory adjustment, for in later years Portia regularly referred to her as "Mama," and the relationship between them was cordial enough.

One page from a pocket notebook kept by Washington shortly before his marriage to Margaret Murray gives a rare bit of insight into his feelings. In the notebook were countless miscellaneous jottings about everything from laundry slips and Sunday School absentees to toothbrushes and chapel seats — notes he had made in his everyday rounds of the campus. Then came the cryptic entry, written in his characteristic scrawl:

> Maggie
>
> 1. Poem
> 2. Last summer
> 3. Tell real feelings to Boys
> 4. What an institution I could make with her help
> Let me keep loving.

His point, "What an institution I could make with her help," was well taken, for, like her predecessor, Margaret Washington devoted herself completely to the success of her husband and Tuskegee.

Washington's remarkable and highly developed gifts as a public speaker also contributed substantially to the new role into which the Atlanta address thrust him. At first he memorized his speeches; later he made only brief outline notes, but rarely referred even to these. Zeal for his cause enabled him to submerge all self-consciousness and keep the attention of his audience on what he was saying. Only rarely did conscious attempts at artistry or oratory creep in, and a natural tendency to the informal and conversational saved him from the flowery phrases to which many orators of his time were addicted. He spoke from personal experience and observation, consciously avoiding "the language of books or the statements in quotations from the authors of books."

Like Lincoln, he made very effective use of homespun humor. He liked to tell such stories as the one about an old Negro whom he asked one day to help clean out the henhouse on the recently purchased Varner farm. "Sho'ly, boss," came the old man's incredulous reply, "you ain't gwine clean out de henhouse in de daytime!" Quick wit made him a master of repartee, enabling him to keep an audience shaking with laughter at his exchanges from the platform. His only idiosyncrasy on the rostrum was an ever-present pencil which he held in his hand, a relic of youthful attempts to learn proper and forceful gestures while speaking.

The invitation to address the annual meeting of the National Education Association in the summer of 1884, when Tuskegee was only three years old, gave Washington his first opportunity to speak before a large national audience. Nearly four thousand people, representing all sections of the country, were present. He approached the platform with fear and trembling, but left it feeling that "in some measure my effort had not been a failure." The fact that he immediately began to receive invitations to speak all over the country led him to say that the Madison address was, in a sense, the beginning of his public-speaking career.

The address was also significant as his first tentative attempt to deal with "the broad question of the relations of the races." Though the Atlanta speech of 1895 was to make his reputation, the speech in Madison clearly outlined the structure of his program for dealing with the race problem, and fifteen years later he wrote that he had found no reason for changing his views "on any important point."

The program sketched out at Madison and developed during the ensuing years was grounded in the conviction that the Negro's home was permanently in the South and that any advancement for his race required, "at least to a certain extent," the co-operation of Southern whites.

Firmly and consistently he opposed all solutions based on colonization schemes: "We are going to stay right here in America," he often assured his white audiences, "and live by your side." Nor did he look with favor on continuing attempts to stimulate northward migration, for he believed that the Negro could push his way upward more easily through Southern prejudice than through Northern competition.

His belief that the Negro was better off in the South could be traced partly to a distinct antiurban prejudice. In too many cases, the black man was "at his worst" in large cities, "and especially the large cities of the North." Conversely, he felt, "One finds the best and more hopeful type of Negroes in the rural districts of the South." The city not only tempted a man to indulge in such vices as gambling, drinking, and immorality, but also — and to Washington this was almost in the same class — to waste his money. It was a place, he told a Harlem audience good-naturedly, where the store windows were so enticing that "the dollars almost jump out of your pockets as you go by." Worst of all, going to the city meant leaving the land for an unstable existence as a wage laborer. Buy land, he always dinned into the ears of his hearers at Tuskegee; if you can't buy a hundred acres, buy thirty; if you can't buy thirty, buy ten; if you can't buy ten, buy one acre and make a beginning.

He further believed in a solidarity of interests between the two races in the South. Both races were engaged in a struggle to adjust themselves to new conditions produced by the war; the welfare of each meant the welfare of the other; and anything he did for his own people would be of no real value to them if it did not benefit the whites by whom they were surrounded. Washington shared the conviction of virtually all white Southerners that the people of the North did not fully understand the paradoxical relationship between white and black in the South. He felt confident that "deep down in their hearts the Southern white people had a feeling of gratitude toward the Negro race" and in the long run would support any "sound and sincere effort" to help.

Though he insisted that "there should be no unmanly cowering or stooping to satisfy the unreasonable whims of Southern white men," his belief that Southern white cooperation was necessary to Negro advancement meant that his policy rested inevitably on accommodation to existing conditions and prejudices. This did not disturb him because, having accepted the social Darwinism of the time, he was convinced that progress for the Negro must come "through no process of artificial forcing, but through the natural law of evolution." The Negro would eventually secure "all the recognition which his merits entitle him to as a man and as a citizen," but "during the next half century and more" he must continue to pass through "the severe American crucible."

He also accepted the corollary doctrine of inevitable progress. "Progress, progress is the law of God," he exclaimed, "and under Him it is going to be the Negro's guiding star in this country." The trend was "ever onward and upward." "One might as well try to stop the progress of a mighty railroad train by throwing his body across the track," he confidently asserted, as to try to arrest the "ceaseless advance of humanity."

If society were moving forward under "well-defined natural laws," then to tamper with the process was not only

useless, but harmful. This analysis reinforced another conviction: that the basis of race advancement must be economic and moral rather than political. The mere fiat of
law, he maintained, "cannot make a dependent man an
independent man; cannot make one citizen respect another. These results will come . . . by beginning at the
bottom and gradually working up."

The Madison speech of 1884 contained a pointed statement of this lack of confidence in political remedies. A
year before, the Supreme Court had declared unconstitutional the Civil Rights Act of 1875 designed to assure
equal enjoyment of the accommodations and privileges of
inns, conveyances, theaters, and places of public amuse-
ment. The Court decision had produced alarm and near
despair among many Negroes who saw in it a complete
reversal of the "favorable sentiment" which had prevailed
in the nation's capital since the war. To Washington, however, it proved that "good schoolteachers and plenty of
money to pay them will be more potent in settling the
race question than many civil rights bills and investigating
committees." "Brains, property, and character" were far
more useful weapons than statutes. Most important of all
was economic progress: "At the bottom of education, at
the bottom of politics, even at the bottom of religion itself," he asserted, "there must be for our race, as for all
races, an economic foundation, economic prosperity, economic independence."

Another principle, that the Negro must rely mainly on
himself, sprang directly from the traditional Puritan gospel of work, admixed with Emersonian self-reliance and
the popular doctrine of "self-help" which the new industrialism had glorified. Mrs. Ruffner and Mary Mackie

had instilled in Washington an everlasting disdain for the idler and the drifter. "In a rich and prosperous country like America," he told his students at Tuskegee, "there is absolutely no excuse for persons living in idleness. I have little patience with persons who go round whining that they cannot find anything to do." Nothing irritated him like the sight of Negro citizens sitting comfortably in the sun around the county courthouse, absorbed in idle gossip.

The Negro's reputation for idleness was understandable, however. Since for years he had been "worked" and had gotten the impression that labor was unmanly, self-reliance and the dignity of labor were at the heart of the Tuskegee program: "We ask help for nothing that we can do for ourselves. . . . A *chance* to help himself is what we want to give to every student." Quoting Carlyle's appeal for "an original man; not a secondhand, borrowing, or begging man," Washington said he was "most anxious" that the Negro be "himself, not a second- or third-rate imitation of someone else." Ever since emancipation the Negro had looked to the Union Army, to the Freedmen's Bureau, to the federal government, to Northern friends for aid and protection. None could solve his problem for him. All he asked now was a "fair chance." Educate the black man "mentally and industrially," Washington promised at Madison, and he would take care of his own future.

The Madison address greatly enhanced Washington's reputation in educational circles and opened the door for appeals on behalf of Tuskegee throughout the Northern states. The same year General Armstrong invited his protégé to join him in a series of meetings designed to raise funds for the two institutions; as Washington found after he gratefully accepted, the meetings turned out to be largely for Tuskegee.

Despite the fact that Washington had access to almost any Northern platform and was rapidly building support among individuals and philanthropic organizations, it was some time before he was able to break through the restrictions of custom to speak to an important white audience in the South. The opportunity finally came in 1893, when he received an invitation to address an international meeting of Christian workers in Atlanta. Since the organization had heard a full report on Tuskegee at its meeting the previous year in a Northern city, Washington's invitation specified that he should confine his remarks to five minutes. He already had engagements in Boston both before and after the time set for the Atlanta meeting, but was reluctant to decline what looked like an opening wedge for direct appeals to the white South. After some hesitation he accepted. The train from Boston put him in Atlanta thirty minutes before he went to the platform; thirty minutes later he boarded the train for the return trip.

As a result of the very favorable reception of his brief speech Washington received an invitation two years later to join a group of Georgia citizens in petitioning Congress for aid to the Cotton States and International Exposition planned for Atlanta the next autumn. He was one of three Negroes (the other two were Methodist bishops) in the delegation of about twenty-five dignitaries. Though he was the last to speak before the Congressional committee, his fifteen-minute appeal made a strong impression. Emphasizing his conviction that property, industry, and character offered the Negro the best chance for improving his status, he pointed out that by aiding the Atlanta project, Congress would "present an opportunity to both races to show what advance they had made since freedom, and would at the same time afford encouragement to them to make still greater progress." After the hearings the committee voted unanimously to recommend the appropriation, and Congress duly passed the bill.

As plans for the exposition progressed, its officials decided to include a building designed by Negroes to house the Negro exhibits. Though they issued the invitation with some misgiving "on account of the fear that public sentiment was not prepared for such an advanced step," they asked Washington to make one of the opening-day addresses. He fully recognized both the opportunity and the responsibility involved, for this was the first time a Negro in the South had been asked to take so prominent a part in a nonpolitical affair of such magnitude. What he said could vitally affect his own future, the future of his school, and quite possibly the future of his race. This seemed to be the time and place, "without condemning what had been done, to emphasize what ought to be done." He had the opportunity to offer a program "not of destruction, but of construction, not of defense, but of aggression; a policy not of hostility or surrender, but of friendship and advance."

Only a short time before the speech a white farmer of the Tuskegee area said to him good-naturedly, "Washington, you have spoken with success before Northern white audiences, and before Negroes in the South, but in Atlanta you will have to speak before Northern white people, Southern white people and Negroes altogether. I fear they have got you into a pretty tight place." Washington had no illusions about the difficulties involved. However, he had made up his mind on two fundamental points: that he would "be perfectly frank and honest" and that he would "not depend upon any 'short cuts' or expedience merely for the sake of gaining temporary popularity or advantage." He was determined "not to say anything that would give undue offense to the South and thus prevent it from thus honoring another Negro in the future," and yet "to be true to the North and to the interests of my own race."

As the day of the exposition drew near, his heart grew heavy with fear that the address would prove "a disappointment and a failure." He went over it carefully with Maggie, as he called his wife, and she approved. When the Tuskegee faculty asked to hear it, he gave them a preview, and was encouraged by their reaction. But he still felt the pangs of anxiety when he, Mrs. Washington, and the children boarded the train for Atlanta on September 17.

They arrived to find the city "delirious with excitement and joy," as one reporter described it. From twenty-five to fifty thousand out-of-town visitors — no one could get an accurate count — jammed hotels and public facilities as the entire town eagerly awaited the next day's opening of the exposition. Victor Herbert's band was to play, the governor, the mayor, and other celebrities would speak, and to cap the climax President Cleveland would press an electric button in Buzzards Bay, Massachusetts, to set the machinery in operation. For those who feared a threat to propriety in such a fever pitch of frivolity and excitement, the press had assured the public that "everything will be highly and aggressively moral."

The next day, with a "booming of cannon, blowing of

whistles, the noise of revolving machinery, the playing of inspiring music by numerous bands, and the applause of thousands of friends and well-wishers," the exposition got under way. After a parade of several hours through the city streets under a broiling September sun, the procession of dignitaries reached the building in which the formal opening exercises were to be held. An immense crowd had packed the hall, and thousands who could not get in milled around the outside. The sight of a tall, heavy-set Negro mounting the speaker's platform, uncommon as the occurrence was, occasioned no surprise, for the press had heralded for several days the fact that Booker T. Washington was to deliver one of the addresses of the occasion. As he took his seat, cheering broke out, mainly from the colored portion of the audience, for of the white listeners some had come out of genuine interest, some out of curiosity, and others in frank expectation of seeing Washington make a fool of himself. One of Washington's white friends was so nervous he could not bring himself to listen, but paced back and forth outside the building until the address was over.

Washington's turn came after several preliminary addresses. The audience waited expectantly as he rose to speak. Before them on the platform, according to the correspondent of the New York *World,* they saw "a remarkable figure, tall, bony, straight as a Sioux chief, high forehead, straight mouth, with big white teeth, piercing eyes, and a determined manner. The sinews stood out on his bronzed neck, and his muscular right arm swung high in the air, with a lead pencil grasped in the clenched brown fist. His big feet were planted squarely, with the heels together and the toes turned out. His voice rang out clear and true, and he paused impressively as he made each point. Within ten minutes the multitude was in an uproar of enthusiasm, handkerchiefs waved, canes flourished, hats tossed in the air. The fairest women in Georgia stood up and cheered. It was as if the orator had bewitched them."

Most of what Washington said he had been saying for years. He stressed again the solidarity of interest between Negro and white man in the South, re-emphasized his belief in a gradual, evolutionary approach, and reasserted his conviction that the Negro must help himself through economic development rather than political agitation. But the address was new in two ways. First, he talked specifically about social equality, a matter he had not mentioned before. Second, he consciously attempted to set forth in integrated fashion what the South, and the entire nation, had been searching for — a practical program of Negro-white relationships.

With the exception of one aside in which he paid his respects to Northern philanthropists for their "constant stream of blessing and encouragement," Washington aimed his speech pointedly at the white South. This was true even of the sections ostensibly addressed to the Negro, for they were primarily designed to reveal the kind of advice he had been giving, and would continue to give, to his own race.

One by one he allayed the fears of Southern whites on the points which disturbed them most. Of the Negro and politics, he disarmingly admitted that serious errors had marked the period of political reconstruction: "Ignorant and inexperienced, it is not strange that in the first years of our new life we began at the top instead of at the bottom; that a seat in Congress or the State Legislature was more sought than real estate or industrial skill; that the political convention or stump speaking had more attraction than starting a dairy farm or truck garden." In the vital realm of labor, he eased Southern minds troubled by migration of Negroes to other areas by urging the members of his race to remain at home, for "it is in the South that the Negro is given a man's chance in the commercial world."

He eliminated the bogey of "social equality" by assuring his audience that "the wisest among my race understand that the agitation of questions of social equality is the extremest folly, and that progress in the enjoyment of all the privileges that will come to us must be the result of severe and constant struggle rather than of artificial forcing." To illustrate his point he thrust his outstretched hand above his head and declared, in one of the most striking figures of speech in American oratory, "In all things that are purely social we can be as separate as the fingers" — and here he brought his fingers together into a solid fist — "yet one has the hand in all things essential to mutual progress."

Then, using one of the down-to-earth figures for which he was famous, he counseled the black man to "cast down your bucket where you are. . . . Cast it down in agriculture, mechanics, in commerce, in domestic service, and in the professions," remembering that "we shall prosper in proportion as we learn to dignify and glorify common labor and put brains and skill into the common occupations of life." The white man for his part should also cast down *his* bucket — "among the eight million Negroes whose habits you know, whose fidelity and love you have tested in days when to have proved treacherous meant the ruin of your firesides . . . among these people who have without strikes and labor wars tilled your fields, cleared your forests, builded your railroads and cities, brought forth treasures from the bowels of the earth." In return for aid, encouragement, and "education of head, hand, and heart," the Negro people would "buy your surplus land, make blossom the waste places in your fields, and run your factories." The white man would then be surrounded "by the most patient, faithful, law-abiding, and unresentful people that the world has seen."

Finally, he pleaded for the higher good, above and beyond the material progress represented by the exposition, which would come "in a blotting out of sectional differences and racial animosities and suspicions, in a determination to administer absolute justice, in a willing obedience among all classes to the mandates of law. This, coupled with our material prosperity, will bring into our beloved South a new heaven and a new earth."

Hardly had he finished speaking when the governor rushed across the stage to grasp his hand, a demonstration which brought another great shout from the audience. The enthusiasm of the crowd was so great that Washington had difficulty in getting out of the building and away from the exposition grounds. Supporters stopped him on every street corner to shake his hand, and on his return trip to Alabama the next day crowds waited at almost every railway station.

As the press in all parts of the country hailed the epochal event, he skyrocketed into national prominence. Clark Howell, editor of the Atlanta *Constitution,* wired to New York that the address "was one of the most notable speeches, both as to character and as to the warmth of its reception, ever delivered to a Southern audience." "The whole speech," Howell added, "is a platform upon which blacks and whites can stand with full justice to each other." Papers from New York to San Francisco, from Richmond to New Orleans, echoed this praise, as did Negro journals like the Richmond *Planet*. President Cleveland wrote to Washington in his own hand, "I thank you with much enthusiasm for making the address. I have read it with intense interest, and I think the Exposition would be fully justified if it did not do more than furnish the opportunity for its delivery." Only a few Negroes, distrustful of any program so palatable to Southern whites, shook their heads and refused to accept Washington as the spokesman for his race.

Coming at a time when leadership in the former Confederate states was passing from the paternalistic former slaveholders to the anti-Negro lower-class whites, the Atlanta speech was an obvious attempt to strike a practical bargain which would protect the Negro's effort to find economic security. Washington offered on behalf of the Negro to renounce agitation for such political nostrums as the Civil Rights Act. He also renounced demands for "social equality," whatever that phrase was interpreted to mean. The Negro agreed to accept, for the time being, the place assigned to him by Southern custom; he would begin at the bottom and strive to make himself worthy of the rights and privileges of full citizenship.

Washington asked in return that the Negro be judged not by his color, but by his worth as an individual human being, and that he be treated accordingly. Primarily,

Washington wanted assurance of equal economic opportunity — the right of the Negro to compete with the white man on even terms, not only in agriculture but in the cotton mills and other industrial plants which were rising in the "New South." This is what he meant by asking that the Negro be given a chance, as he developed, to buy the white man's surplus land, make blossom the waste places in his fields, and run his factories. He also hoped, if the Negro should fulfill his part of the bargain, that the white man would "blot out" race prejudice and administer absolute justice which did not take into account the color of a man's skin.

To Washington it seemed that he was not giving up much in such a compromise. Political remedies had failed, and "social equality" had become more a shibboleth than a tangible goal; to exchange them for the guarantee of equal economic opportunity was a common-sense choice between "the superficial and the substantial."

Unfortunately, however, fulfillment of the bargain depended on the enlightenment of a white South thoroughly conditioned in its ideas about the Negro by the master-slave relationship and the experience of Reconstruction. Washington occasionally had a tendency to ambiguity at points where ambiguity was least desirable; consequently the Southern white man was able to interpret his program in such a way as to accept more than Washington meant to offer, and to miss entirely the fact that a *quid pro quo* was involved. For example, the statement that "it is more important that we be prepared to vote than that we vote" could easily be stretched to mean that Washington had no great objection to disfranchisement of the Negro. The assertion that "we shall prosper as we learn to dignify and glorify common labor" the white man could interpret as permanent acceptance of a servile status. Even so astute an observer as Clark Howell missed the emphasis on the word "agitation" in the statement that "the agitation of questions of social equality is the extremest folly," and failed to discern that Washington looked forward to a time when the Negro would be accorded this and other rights. Finally, the white man could place a very loose construction on the phrase "in all things purely social." As increasing segregation laws were to show, the Negro was to find the two races "as separate as the fingers" in many areas which were not "purely social" at all.

Most significantly, the Atlanta speech helped to establish the "separate but equal" principle as the yardstick in American race relations for half a century or more. Washington had used that very phrase, in reverse, as early as the Madison speech, when he praised the railroad commissioners of Alabama for ordering "equal but separate" accommodations for white and Negro passengers. He praised them because their action helped to remedy the inexcusable discrimination to which Negroes had been subjected, but he seemed also to agree with the press accounts which characterized the solution as "just." The Atlanta speech was interpreted to mean that the Negro would accept the "separate but equal" principle. The very next year, in 1896, the Supreme Court of the United States cemented this doctrine into the law of the land.

As a result of his Atlanta address, lecture agents besieged Washington with offers which would have netted him a small personal fortune. He brushed them aside on

the ground that they would interfere with his work at
Tuskegee. As time went on, he accepted engagements
booked by professional agencies, but only when he was
allowed to appeal directly for his school; and the money
invariably went back into the Tuskegee treasury. A genuinely unselfish person, he was mindful of the Biblical injunction as to the root of all evil and seems to have had
no desire for a personal fortune. Few things upset him as
much as Andrew Carnegie's wish, some years later, to set
up a trust fund which would have given Washington a substantial personal income.

He did, however, take advantage of his new position to
further the interests of Tuskegee. The autumn of 1895
found him speaking to large audiences in Massachusetts,
New York, Pennsylvania, and the Midwest. While in Chicago as the guest of the Hamilton Club, an influential Republican organization, he was invited by the president of
the University of Chicago to address the students there,
and a similar invitation from Trinity College of Durham,
North Carolina, gave him his first opportunity to talk to
white college students in the South.

In June, 1896, President Eliot of Harvard conferred on
him the honorary degree of Master of Arts, the first time
Harvard had so honored a Negro. The following autumn,
following McKinley's election, the Washington *Post* urged
the President-elect to consider Washington for his Cabinet, suggesting that the post of Secretary of Agriculture
would be appropriate. A good many journals took up the
matter, and for a short time it became a live issue. Washington confided to a friend late in December that while he
was "getting a lot of fun out of the Cabinet matter" and
had let friends go ahead with it thinking it would do the

race no harm, "Mr. McKinley has no position within his gift that I would think of accepting were it offered." Shortly thereafter he put an end to the talk by stating publicly he could not accept an appointment which would take him from his work at Tuskegee.

V I I

Widening Circles of Influence

By COINCIDENCE, Frederick Douglass, recognized for years as the foremost Negro in America, died only a few months before Washington's Atlanta speech. It was only natural for Washington to be hailed as his successor. The Tuskegee educator greatly admired Douglass, claiming that the essence of the Tuskegee doctrine came directly from the older man, who in his later years counseled the Negro to stay in the South, develop industrial schools, and acquire property. Douglass also admired Tuskegee; he had delivered the commencement address in 1892, and a few weeks before his death had written to Washington in praise of his "great and leading educational institution."

A few persons, to whom the line of descent from Douglass to Washington seemed very tenuous, refused to recognize the succession of the new leader, but their objections went unheard. Because he accommodated himself and his program with such remarkable success to the conditions of time and place, it became the accepted custom for everyone from the President of the United States down to consult Washington on any matter involving the Negro. His new prestige took him into the most fashionable parlors of Boston and New York; he became the friend of the great and near great, readily absorbing the dominant business philosophy of the circles in which he now moved. As his personal stature increased, so did the stature of his school. The growth of Tuskegee and the greatly multiplied demands on the principal's time meant that he had to have more help.

Of the many persons added to his staff after the early years, the two most important were George Washington Carver and Emmett J. Scott. Carver, whose fame, in the fields of chemistry and scientific agriculture, was to rival Washington's own, went to Tuskegee in 1896 at the age of thirty-three as head of the agricultural-training program. Born a slave, he had shown as a boy not only an interest in and love for plant life, but also talent in art and music. Eventually, after making his living as a greenhouse worker and as a church organist, he found his way to Iowa State College at Ames, where he earned the first postgraduate degree given by that institution. One of his teachers, James Wilson, who served as Secretary of Agriculture under McKinley, Roosevelt, and Taft, called Carver to the attention of Washington, who wrote to him early in 1896 about coming to Tuskegee.

Carver was drawn to Tuskegee because he believed that its type of education was "the key to unlock the golden door of freedom" to his people. He shared Washington's strong sense of mission, religious faith, and ideas on race. He made possible a tremendous advance in agricultural training and also the extension of Tuskegee's influence throughout Alabama and the South by improved farm methods.

What Carver meant to the institution Emmett Scott meant to Washington personally. A Howard University graduate and editor of the *Texas Freeman,* Scott first attracted attention at Tuskegee by warm praise of the Atlanta address; two years later he handled arrangements for Washington's visit to Houston. Badly needing help with his flood of correspondence, Washington approached Scott about joining his staff, and in 1897 the former journalist became his private secretary.

From the day Scott arrived, when Washington pushed toward him a pile of diversified correspondence with the casual remark, "I wish you would dispose of these letters as rapidly as possible," the new secretary was a trusted and intimate associate. Soon made secretary of the Institute, he became the principal's confidential adviser and alter ego. This close relationship lasted until Washington's death in 1915, but even Scott never addressed him except as "Mr. Washington."

Another important addition to the Tuskegee administrative staff was Monroe N. Work, grandson of a slave who had bought his own freedom and that of his wife and ten children. Work arrived at Tuskegee to head the new Records and Research Department, which had been created to handle requests for information from all over the United States and other countries. Some of these came from high school boys and girls seeking debate material; others asked Washington's opinion on every imaginable question; still others came from people in all walks of life who wanted information about Tuskegee or about various phases of Negro life. Monroe Work's conscientious handling of this department helped to free Washington for more important tasks.

Addition of staff members to whom he could delegate some phases of his work did not mean that Washington relinquished for a moment his personal direction of Tuskegee. Insisting that he be informed of every detail of the school's operation, he worked out a series of forms on which each department head reported daily; any offender who did not submit his report by 8:30 A.M. received a prompt rebuke from the principal's office. The information gleaned from these reports he reinforced by personal tours of observation, notebook and pencil in hand. Nothing seems to have escaped his eye. "I hope that you will see that the whitewashing of the farm fences is kept regularly and systematically up," he would write to a subordinate, adding characteristically, "I wish you would report to me what plan you have for doing this." Even during his absences from Tuskegee the school was still on his mind. Staff members would often get notes such as one written from New York in 1903: "I hope that you will find out at once some way of lowering the alarming death rate among the hogs. This matter is getting entirely too serious."

Though this type of personal direction continued throughout Washington's life, the growth of Tuskegee meant a steady increase in his public-relations work on behalf of the institution. Money was a problem which dogged his footsteps till the day of his death. During his last years, faced with the necessity of finding more than $100,000 annually to balance the budget, he spent as much as two thirds of his time cultivating Northern philanthropists and foundations. Fortunately, large sums were flowing from Northern coffers to the aid of Southern education, and Washington saw to it that a considerable proportion found its way to Tuskegee.

Hardly was Tuskegee Institute under way in the early 1880's before Washington successfully appealed to two funds established to encourage education in the South. Recognizing the great need which the chaos and dislocation of the Civil War left in its wake, the merchant and financier George Peabody had set up in 1867 a fund of two and a half million dollars "for the promotion and encouragement of intellectual, moral, or industrial education among the young people of the more destitute portions of the Southern and Southwestern States." In 1882 the textile magnate John F. Slater, stimulated by the success of the Peabody Fund, gave one million dollars for the specific purpose of educating Negroes. During the early years of Tuskegee Institute both the Peabody and Slater funds were administered by J. L. M. Curry, a prominent white Southerner with whom Washington established a warm friendship. Beginning with the year 1883, Tuskegee received the first of a number of gifts from each of these foundations.

More important, Washington succeeded in gaining the confidence and support of an increasing number of Northern industrialists and financiers. The Atlanta speech gave great impetus to his fund-raising efforts, as did the publication of *Up From Slavery* in 1900. *Up From Slavery* was his second attempt at an autobiography; shortly before, he had completed *The Story of My Life and Work,* a disjointed collection of newspaper articles, speeches, and letters connected by a narrative of Washington's life. This book made little impression. When the editors of *Outlook* approached him in 1900 for a serialized version of his life, he hesitated, mainly, his secretary wrote later, because "he could not believe that the events of his life would be of any interest to the public." He did undertake the task, however, writing installments whenever and wherever he could, often on scraps of paper in railroad stations, on trains, and in hotels.

Published in book form after its appearance in the *Outlook*, the simple, direct, dramatic *Up From Slavery* immediately became a best seller. It was a Horatio Alger novel with a new twist, the true rags-to-riches story of a black boy who had risen from the social level of the slave cabin to acceptance at the Court of St. James — and shortly thereafter, at the White House. It appealed to foreign readers as well and soon enjoyed the distinction of being translated into more languages than any other American book of its time. Several of the institution's most affluent and beneficent friends became interested in Tuskegee as a direct result of reading it, and by 1915 it had brought more money to the Institute than all the rest of Washington's speeches, articles, and books combined.

Neither the Atlanta speech nor *Up From Slavery*, however, could have produced the results which flowed from Washington's personal efforts. That he was an expert in public relations even his enemies freely admitted. One of his principal tactics he borrowed directly from General Armstrong: he regularly made it a practice to "plow out a hole, pile the bricks and lumber around," and bring a party of businessmen from the North. He rightly discerned that an appeal to such men on the campus of Tuskegee, where they could see for themselves the achievements and the needs of the institution, would bring in ten times more than an interview in a New York office. During the first decade of the new century he developed this technique so successfully that Robert C. Ogden, general manager for John Wanamaker, and Seth Low, mayor of New York, undertook the organization of annual visits to Tuskegee by parties of influential Easterners. John Wanamaker himself financed the special trains for these pilgrimages. Later the idea was copied by Julius Rosenwald, who brought friends from the Midwest to Tuskegee.

On such occasions Washington mobilized the energies of both students and teachers to put on the most impressive display possible. His most striking public-relations venture before 1900 was his success in persuading President McKinley to visit Tuskegee in December, 1898. A crowd of six thousand people, including the governor and the state legislature en masse, turned out to welcome the President and Mrs. McKinley, the members of his Cabinet, and several generals who had earned their fame in the Spanish-American War. After the President reached the speakers' stand, the entire student body of Tuskegee passed in review before him, each carrying a stalk of sugar cane with open bolls of cotton fastened to the end of it; following the students came an hour-and-a-half parade of floats exhibiting the work of the vocational-training departments. After this demonstration the crowd moved into the newly completed chapel for McKinley's address, in which he warmly endorsed Washington's "noble enterprise."

The Tuskegee commencement exercises, which annually attracted eight to nine thousand people, also gave Washington an opportunity to keep the work of the school before the public. "On the platform before the audience," wrote Emmett Scott of a typical commencement, "is a miniature engine to which steam has been piped, a miniature frame house in course of construction, and a piece of brick wall in process of erection. A young man in jumpers comes onto the platform, starts the engine, and blows the whistle, whereupon young men and women come hurrying from all directions, and each turns to his or her appointed task. . . . At the same time on the opposite side of the platform one of the girl students is having a dress fitted by one of her classmates who is a dressmaker. . . . Other girls are doing washing and ironing with the drudgery removed in accordance with advanced Tuskegee methods. . . . In the background are arranged the finest specimens which scientific agriculture has produced on the farm and mechanical skill has turned out in the shops."

A year after President McKinley's visit to Tuskegee, Washington launched in Madison Square Garden a campaign for a large permanent endowment for Tuskegee. The roster of those who attended read like a roll call of New York's upper crust. Former President Cleveland, prevented by a last-minute illness from presiding, sent a letter of encouragement and an offer by an anonymous donor of $25,000. On the platform and in the boxes were such men as Robert Ogden, Walter Hines Page, Seth Low, Levi P. Morton, Nicholas Murray Butler, Carl Schurz, Collis P. Huntington, August Belmont, Jacob H. Schiff, W. H. Baldwin, Jr., Cleveland H. Dodge, Lyman Abbott, J. Pierpont Morgan, and John D. Rockefeller. It is hardly surprising that with such support the campaign got off to a good start. Rockefeller contributed $10,000, Huntington $50,000, and four years later Andrew Carnegie, who had already given Tuskegee a library, tripled the endowment by a gift of $600,000 in U. S. Steel bonds. By the time of

Washington's death the fund had reached approximately two million dollars, an endowment larger than that of virtually all Southern colleges, white or Negro.

The interest of men of wealth and position in an enterprise like Tuskegee grew out of a fortuitous combination of circumstances. The new industrialism, with its great concentrations of wealth, had brought with it an era of increased philanthropy based on the Protestant doctrine of stewardship. The South, still struggling to recoup its losses of the Civil War period, offered a logical outlet for benevolences, and it behooved the victorious North to offer its resources. To help the South was also good business, for Northern firms desired a trained, stable labor force and a higher level of prosperity which would contribute to expanding markets.

Washington appealed to Northern businessmen not only because of his forceful personal qualities, but also because he was a self-made man in the best American tradition. The Puritan strain in his background had molded a sense of values out of the same heritage from which theirs were derived. Partly because of his association with them he hewed, as they did, to the conservative line in politics, religion, and economics. He accepted their gospel of wealth as elaborated by Andrew Carnegie. Like them, he was critical of organized labor, pointing out to white audiences that the Negro was not given to strikes and the fomenting of labor troubles.

His resentment against unions and "professional labor agitators" did not spring from opposition to organized labor in principle. He himself had belonged to the Knights of Labor for several years during his life in West Virginia and believed that unions could and would become an important means of eliminating racial prejudice. But he bitterly resented the "Lily-white" attitudes, prevalent in the American Federation of Labor and other unions, which had precipitated fifty strikes during the 1880's and 1890's for the purpose of freezing out colored workers. In assailing this kind of "cowardice and prejudice," he exercised little of his usual moderation. "We have had slavery, now dead, that forced an individual to labor without a salary," he observed caustically, "but none that compelled a man to remain in idleness while his family starved." A color line in labor struck at the one right Washington considered fundamental to the Negro's advancement: the right to economic opportunity, and it did so at a time when the Negro was having difficulty maintaining his hold even on jobs which had been allocated to him by tradition.

Whatever Washington's motives, his lack of sympathy with the labor movement coincided with that of men from whom he drew his support and helped to cement the bonds of a natural collaboration between them. As his work brought him into contact with a widening circle of influential persons, he developed poise and an ease of manner which enabled him to mingle with them on even terms. Eventually he felt completely at home on the yacht of Henry H. Rogers of Standard Oil, whom he knew, according to his own testimony, as well as anyone outside his family. He became an intimate of the railroad builders William H. Baldwin, Jr., and Collis Huntington, and visited Andrew Carnegie at Skibo Castle. He also numbered among his friends and admirers college presidents like Eliot of Harvard, editors like Lyman Abbott and Walter Hines Page, and ministers like Phillips Brooks and

Charles M. Sheldon. William James assured him that he was counted on "to save the country," and H. G. Wells invited Washington to be his house guest in England.

As they came to know Washington, Northern philanthropists interested in Southern education began to look to him for advice. In 1902, mainly as a result of events set in motion by the Tuskegee head, John D. Rockefeller established and endowed the General Education Board for the improvement of higher learning, directing that it give particular attention to the South and to institutions for Negroes. As a director of the board, Washington worked closely for years with its active head, Wallace Buttrick. In co-operation with Hollis Frissell, General Armstrong's successor at Hampton, he was also responsible for establishing the Anna T. Jeanes Fund for the assistance of Negro rural schools. Washington became chairman of the Jeanes Fund's executive committee and chose its executive director, James H. Dillard. Finally, he played an active part in the founding of the Phelps-Stokes Fund, which took a special interest in the Negro, and in the Negro rural-school program financed by Julius Rosenwald.

Such funds materially aided the extension work which spread the Tuskegee influence in ever-widening circles from its center at the Institute. Washington had always considered Tuskegee a city set on a hill, with responsibilities not only to its students but to the entire Negro race. Out of this conception came his first major extension effort, the annual Tuskegee Negro Conferences which began in 1892. About four hundred Negroes "of all kinds and conditions" responded to his first invitation to come to the school for a day's discussion of their problems. Since Washington was anxious that the program not consist of theoretical advice in lecture form, the proceedings were very informal. He invited members of the audience during the morning session to stand up and report on living conditions, landowning, schools, moral and religious conditions in their own communities. In the afternoon he encouraged the more enterprising to tell how they had freed themselves from debt, what crops they were raising, how many head of livestock they owned, and so forth.

In accordance with Washington's desire for "positive, aggressive effort, rather than mere negative criticisms and recitation of our wrongs," participants in the first conference pledged themselves to work toward tangible goals: to raise their own food, as quickly as possible to buy land, to give their children the opportunity to learn trades, to broaden the field of labor for Negro women, to insist that their ministers and teachers give more attention to the living conditions of their people, and to insure adequate schools by supplementing state funds with money from their own pockets.

These annual gatherings grew immensely in popularity and within a few years attracted more than a thousand people a year. They came on foot, in wagons or buggies, on horseback, by any and every means of conveyance, not only from nearby counties but from nearby states. Many of them took pride in telling how they had heeded Washington's injunction to "make your own little heaven right here and now." One such testimony came from a tall, elderly black man who rose in response to Washington's invitation and said, "Doctor, I done 'tended one o' yore conferences here 'bout ten year ago. I heard you say dat a man ain't wuth nuthin' as a man or a citizen 'less he owns his home, 'least one mule, and has a bank account, an' so I made up my mind dat I warn't wuth nuthin', an' so I went home an' talked de whole matter over wid de ol' woman. We decided dat we would make a start, an' now I's proud to tell you dat I's not only got a bank account, but I's got two bank accounts, an' heah's de bank books [proudly holding on high two grimy bank books]; I also own two hun'ed acres of land an' all de land is paid for. I also own two mules, an' bofe dem mules is paid for. I also own some other property, an' de ole woman an' me an' de chilluns lives in a good house an' de house is paid for. All dis come 'bout from my coming to dis heah conference."

After the arrival of George Washington Carver and the establishment of the State Agricultural Experiment Station at Tuskegee in 1897, attendants at the conferences had as a consultant on farming methods the most distinguished agricultural scientist in the country. Not only Negro but white farmers marveled at Carver's ability to make the land produce. Where they had been digging thirty-seven bushels of sweet potatoes to the acre, he dug two hundred sixty-six bushels. Where the average Southern farmer raised less than two hundred pounds of cotton to the acre, he raised five hundred. The Tuskegee experiment station published a "Farmer's Calendar" advising what to plant and when to plant it, as well as innumerable pamphlets on such subjects as "The Possibilities of the Sweet Potato in Macon County," "How to Grow the Peanut and 105 Ways of Preparing It for Human Consumption," "How to Raise Pigs with Little Money," "When, What, and How to Can and Preserve Fruits and Vegetables in the Home," and "A New and Prolific Variety of Cotton."

For farmers who could not or did not attend the conferences, Washington sent through the countryside wagons drawn by strong, healthy mules, each with a good breed of cow tied behind, and filled with chickens, corn, cotton, oats, garden products, seeds, and a modern plow. The driver would approach a farmer, talk with him, then ask for a strip of ground for cultivation. As the farmer looked on, the driver would plow deep, plant several varieties of seeds, then return later for a follow-up of his practical demonstration. Even more ambitious was the Farmers' Short Course, a two weeks' program of study in modern methods which preceded the annual Negro Conferences. Starting in 1907 with eleven students, the course attracted two thousand by 1913. Largely as a result of Tuskegee's efforts, more than five hundred of the thirty-eight hundred Negro farmers in Macon County owned their farms by 1910, and more than 90 per cent of the total were either owners or cash renters.

Soon after her husband organized the first Negro Conference, Mrs. Washington began looking for ways to help the women of the area, many of whom were more interested than the men in bettering their condition. Noticing that most of them spent their Saturdays in town with little to do, she obtained the loan of a dingy second-floor hall in Tuskegee and sent a little boy out to whisper to women he met on the street, "A woman up those stairs has something for you." Six came, and together they talked of ways of helping themselves and each other. From this beginning grew the weekly Women's Meetings, which eventually attracted three hundred each Saturday. As time went on, Mrs. Washington developed a program covering such subjects as morals among young girls, amusements for children, a mother's duty to the home, dressmaking, poultry raising, and canning of foods.

In addition to the Tuskegee Negro Conferences and the Women's Meetings, Washington provided as many other services as possible for the Negro community. In 1892 he established a dispensary which grew into a $50,000 hospital; from the first it was open to any who were ill, many of whom Washington sent in personally as a result of his trips through the county. He also established a Ministers' Night School for the country clergy, a Building and Loan Association to aid in home building, and a town night school and library for boys and girls in the town of Tuskegee. In 1898 he organized the Negro County Fair as a further incentive to Negro farmers, and in 1904 began an intensive campaign for rural education which resulted in fifty new schools, white and Negro, in Macon County alone. Through this effort Washington built such a sense of pride among rural citizens that they soon looked down on the community which did not have a school with classrooms, rooms for cooking and crafts, and a school garden or farm. Such activities enabled Washington to keep in touch with the common people of the Tuskegee area, and he took pride in what the school was doing for them.

The Tuskegee influence eventually reached far beyond the confines of Macon County. In 1900, at the request of the German Government, J. N. Calloway took three Tuskegee graduates to Africa for the purpose of introducing cotton culture into the colony of Togo. Supplied with tools, a cotton gin, and several varieties of cotton seed, they were so successful that three more Tuskegee graduates joined the project at the end of the second year. As a result of the Togo experiment, British and Belgian authorities requested similar missions for their African possessions. Such ventures gave great impetus to vocational training by foreign missionaries, not only in Africa but elsewhere; Robert E. Speer of the Presbyterian Board of Foreign Missions wrote to Washington in 1902 that he was receiving requests from missionaries in China asking for the introduction of "industrial education" of the Tuskegee type.

Though Tuskegee's extension work was designed primarily for the rural Negro, Washington's interest in any project which would stimulate Negro enterprise led to the founding of the National Negro Business League in 1900. Impressed with the number of successful Negro entrepreneurs he met during his travels about the country, he became convinced that an organization which would bring these men together for exchange of ideas and mutual inspiration would be of great value to the race. He talked the matter over with Scott and with T. Thomas Fortune, editor of the New York *Age,* who was spending the winter of 1900 at Tuskegee. They decided that local leagues could supplement the work of the national organization by aiding in the employment of Negroes, protecting consumers against worthless products and fraudulent schemes, fostering an interest in civic welfare, and creating race pride.

Approximately four hundred Negro bankers, realtors, grocers, merchants, caterers, manufacturers, contractors, druggists, undertakers, bakers, printers, restaurateurs, barbers, plumbers, milliners, dressmakers, jewelers, and publishers gathered in Boston for the first meeting of the Business League in 1900. Though the group was more sophisticated than that which attended the Tuskegee Negro Conference, the program also consisted mainly of success stories by the delegates. Great applause greeted the testimony of a delegate from Florida who related that nineteen years before he had gone to Jacksonville with a dollar and ten cents in his pocket and a suit of underwear in a paper bag — "and today I pay more taxes than any Negro in Florida." As could have been expected, a sober, practical atmosphere prevailed; politics and protest had no place in the meeting.

By 1905 the league's three hundred local affiliates had reached into all the urban centers where Negroes were concentrated. John Wanamaker, Robert C. Ogden, and Oswald Garrison Villard, editor of the New York *Evening Post*, lent importance to the organization by addressing its annual meeting of that year, and Theodore Roosevelt performed the same function five years later. From the league grew such offshoots as the National Negro Funeral Directors' Association, the Negro Bar Association, the Colored Merchants' Association, and the National Association of Negro Insurance Men. For fifteen years Washington served as president of the Business League and, with the aid of Emmett Scott, personally directed its activities.

The existence of the Business League strengthened Washington's influence and aided the projection of his ideas in urban Negro communities just as the many organizations and services centered at Tuskegee did among Negroes of the rural South. For almost ten years after the Atlanta speech his position was so strong that both his leadership and his program went virtually unchallenged.

V I I I

Spokesman for the Race

INCREASINGLY, as practical issues involving Negro-white relationships arose on the state and national level, Washington was forced to put to the test the philosophy of race relations enunciated at Atlanta. As the acknowledged leader of his fellows, he could not ignore such questions as the movement for Negro disfranchisement which began in the 1890's or the alarming number of lynchings which filled the front pages of the newspapers; nor could he easily avoid being drawn into politics when government officials from the President down regularly sought his advice on political appointments. Such influence and activity inevitably provoked an opposition which smoldered during the years following 1895 and broke into flame ten years later.

Attempts to deprive the Negro of the ballot by legal devices began in Mississippi in 1890 and within the decade became an issue throughout the Southern states. This stemmed in part from the reaction of the white South against the radical application of pure democracy which the gift of the franchise to the Negro represented. By the turn of the century Pitchfork Ben Tillman was able to say on the floor of the United States Senate — and get away with it — that after the removal of federal troops from South Carolina in 1876 the whites "rose in righteousness and right. We took the government; we stuffed the ballot boxes; we bulldozed the niggers and we shot 'em. And we are not ashamed of it. The people of South Carolina, in their Constitution, have done their level best to prevent the niggers from voting."

Even in South Carolina, however, there was no real unity among the white citizens. In most Southern states the disfranchisement movement resulted also from a struggle for supremacy between the former planters and the lower-class whites, a struggle as old as the Tidewater–back-country conflict of colonial days. In some instances it was an effort by the small-farmer element to wrest control from the "Redeemers" by eliminating the heavy Negro representation through which the former controlled elections. In others, the conservative element pressed for disfranchisement devices to keep the mass of "unfit" white as well as Negro voters from the polls and thereby preserve the *status quo*.

The principal devices invented to limit the franchise were the literacy test and a property qualification, in many cases rigged to discriminate against Negro voters. Mississippi accomplished this by a clause which required an understanding of a given portion of the Constitution; this left to local election officials the decision as to a voter's qualifications, and in practice meant that illiterate whites voted, illiterate Negroes did not. Louisiana invented the more ingenious "grandfather clause" which exempted from literacy and property tests all those entitled to vote on January 1, 1867, together with their sons and grandsons. All states adopted the poll tax as a voting qualification, some adding refinements such as advance payment, the necessity of preserving the tax receipt, and the stipulation that the tax was cumulative.

Washington, agreeing with conservative whites that some form of restricted franchise was desirable, was unwilling to oppose all devices to discourage black voters. Moreover, a clear-cut strategy dictated his actions. Since he considered some degree of disfranchisement inevitable, he wished to salvage as much as possible from the wreckage of the Fifteenth Amendment. Fearing especially blanket legislation which would bar Negroes as a race, regardless of the worth of individuals, he battled primarily to keep the suffrage for the individual Negro who by any reasonable standard could prove himself worthy of exercising his political rights. Washington felt confident that, if this door were kept open, education would eventually qualify the vast majority of his people for full citizenship.

As the rash of disfranchisement efforts spread, Washington tried to counter with direct and indirect methods. His public letter to Senator Tillman, the moving spirit of the South Carolina constitutional convention of 1895, failed to move "Pitchfork Ben," and South Carolina followed Mississippi's lead of five years before. When the Louisiana convention met in 1898, Washington and the Negro editor T. Thomas Fortune sat up all night composing a public appeal. The letter did not succeed in deterring the convention, but it did gain wide support for Washington's moderate position both in Louisiana and elsewhere. In the letter, which is one of the first occasions on which Washington openly presumed to speak for his race, he asserted that the Negro did not object to an educational or property test. But, he said, "let the law be so clear that no one clothed with state authority will be tempted to perjure and degrade himself by putting one interpretation upon it for the white man and another for the black man."

He became "almost disgusted with the colored people in Georgia" when the disfranchisement fever seized that state in 1899, for he could not "stir up a single colored man to take the lead in trying to head off this movement." Finally he went personally to Atlanta and talked with legislators, newsmen, and other influential citizens, stating publicly that he could not believe the Southern white people "want it continually advertised to the world that some special law must be passed by which they will seem to be given an unfair advantage over the Negro."

In Alabama he helped to plan a conference on the franchise which represented varying points of view, and sat unmoved in the balcony reserved for Negroes while John Temple Graves, a well-known Southern newsman, used him to support an argument for "complete separation" of the races. Opposing Graves was the former governor of West Virginia, whom Washington had hand-picked for the occasion in the knowledge that the governor would argue for equal application to both races of any educational or property test. The disfranchisement current was running too strong, however, and Washington's efforts had little effect other than to awaken the conscience of a minority of more thoughtful whites and perhaps to check some of the extremists. By 1910 virtually all Southern Negroes had lost the right to vote.

On lynching, Washington took a less qualified position than on disfranchisement. The practice had reached its peak in 1892, when two hundred thirty-five people were murdered by mobs, but at the turn of the century was still taking the lives of more than a hundred annually. When a rash of particularly brutal lynchings broke out in 1899, Washington was in Europe, having been sent there by Boston friends for his first vacation since 1881. On receiving reports of these lynchings from the United States, Washington was tempted to speak out immediately, but "kept silent, because I did not believe that the public mind was in a condition to listen to a discussion of the subject in the calm judicial manner that it would be later, when there should be no undue feeling or excitement."

On his return from Europe, however, he addressed a widely published letter to the white people of the South. The tone of the letter was "calm" and "judicial." As usual, he appealed to the better nature of the Southern white man, reminding him that the "policy of noninterference" on the part of the federal government imposed on the South a "sacred trust." He professed his love for the South and his concern for everything that involved its welfare, but pointed out that the South must admit responsibility for the vast majority of lynchings.

He went on to disavow any intention of condoning Negro crime. On the contrary, he admitted that because of ignorance and poverty his race was responsible for far more than its proportion of criminal cases, but lynching, he pointed out, did not stop crime. Furthermore, the pretext on which it had begun — as a means of punishing outrages on women — was a fallacy since less than 20 per cent of the lynchings then committed involved even alleged rape. Worst of all, it not only gave the South a reputation for lawlessness which all Southerners deplored, but had a terribly degrading moral effect on the persons involved. "Never shall I forget," he wrote, "the remark by a little nine-year-old white boy, with blue eyes and flaxen hair. The little fellow said to his mother after he had returned from a lynching, 'I have seen a man hanged; now I wish I could see one burned.'" "With the best white people and the best black people standing together, in favor of law and order and justice," he concluded, "I believe that the safety and happiness of both races will be made secure."

In all his pronouncements which implied criticism of the white South, Washington tried to be more than circumspect, believing that moderation and conciliation would gain more in the long run than "extreme utterances." Furthermore, he was constantly aware that an indiscretion might destroy his influence and cause a serious reaction against Tuskegee. His private correspondence shows that in many instances involving discrimination or injustice he could, as he wrote at one time, "hardly keep still." On more than one such occasion he fought undercover with considerable more vehemence than he was willing to show in public; for example, during the running battle on disfranchisement he sent to a friend in Boston a strongly worded letter to be "planted" in the Boston papers under an assumed name. In the letter Washington strongly protested the disfranchisement devices recently adopted by Louisiana and North Carolina and urged that a test case be taken to the Supreme Court to determine their constitutionality. At the same time he was privately giving his support to a fund being raised by Negroes in Washington for the purpose of financing such a test.

Nothing illustrates better the fact that he was continually walking a tight rope in the South than the misstep he made in his speech at the Chicago Peace Jubilee at the end of the Spanish-American War. In his Atlanta speech he had appealed for the higher good that would come "in a blotting out of sectional differences and racial animosities." The Chicago address included almost the same phrase, but Washington made the mistake of substituting the word "prejudices" for "animosities." At the suggestion that prejudice was a "cancer gnawing at the heart of the republic," Southern editors burst out in a fury of protest. The storm grew to such an extent that Washington felt it wise to explain that his remarks had nothing to do with social equality and were directed not at the South alone, but at the entire nation.

In his conduct Washington also tried to avoid offending the white South. Early in his career he consciously adopted a policy of doing as the Romans did. While in the South he conformed to Southern practices and submitted to segregation whenever this did not interfere with his work; outside the South he refused to be bound by Southern custom. He had come to the conclusion, he wrote, that prejudices were curious things which "it does not pay to disturb. It is best to 'let sleeping dogs lie.'"

Even in the North he carefully shunned "purely social" functions, and Mrs. Washington never accompanied him when there was any question as to the nature of the occasion. His contacts with white people were primarily matters of business, either in the interest of Tuskegee or in the interest of the Negro race. "You have no idea," he tried to explain to a friend, "how many invitations of various kinds I am constantly refusing or trying to get away from because I want to avoid embarrassing situations. . . . Of course, if I wanted to make a martyr of myself and draw especial attention to me and to the institution, I could easily do so by simply writing whenever I receive an invitation to a dinner or banquet that I could not accept on account of the color of my skin."

Because of his unique position the South allowed him certain privileges most Negroes did not enjoy. For years he rode Pullman cars without objection from any quarter. On a trip from Augusta to Atlanta he once entered a Pullman where two Boston ladies whom he knew well were sitting. They insisted that he join them, and a few minutes later ordered supper to be served in the car to the three of them. Washington, feeling the eyes of the white men in the car on him, tried without success to contrive some excuse to leave. Finally he settled back in his seat thinking, "I am in for it now, sure." After the meal was over, he excused himself and made his way into the smoking room "to see how the land lay." To his surprise and relief, every man there, most of them Southerners, came up and introduced himself and thanked Washington for the work he was doing at Tuskegee.

The fact that he did enjoy special privileges perhaps led him unsuspectingly into the incident which caused more adverse comment than anything in his career: his dinner at the White House with Theodore Roosevelt in the autumn of 1901. He had little reason to expect the storm which broke over his head. He had dined in the same room with President McKinley only three years before at the Chicago Peace Jubilee and with former President Harrison in Paris; the American Ambassadors to England and France, to say nothing of prominent Englishmen and Frenchmen, had entertained him in their homes. He had even had tea with Queen Victoria. But to white Southerners the entertainment of a Negro at the White House, even though he was Booker T. Washington, was an implied threat to the continuance of segregation.

Washington had embraced the Republican party well before Theodore Roosevelt succeeded to the Presidency. At the time of the election of 1896 he had made no secret of his sympathies, referring to McKinley's victory as "the decision of the great American Jury, that our own country is to go forward and not backward in its business and commercial life." This identification with the party of sound money and general conservatism was the beginning of a lifelong attachment for Washington in spite of his early warning that the Republican party was not composed exclusively of angels and of the Negro's friends. It also laid the foundation for a stanch friendship between Washington and Roosevelt.

Shortly before McKinley's death the Vice-President, with whom Washington was already well acquainted, had been planning a trip South which would have included a visit to Tuskegee. On the day Roosevelt became President he dispatched a letter to Washington regretting that his trip must be postponed and urging Washington to come north instead. "I must see you as soon as possible," he wrote. "I want to talk over the question of possible appointments in the South exactly on the lines of our conversation together."

This letter reached Washington in Mississippi, where he was traveling. He obeyed the impulsive new President's summons with some hesitation, knowing that the delicate matter of appointments meant involvement in political affairs, but he felt that the interests of the race dictated that he go. Within a month he went twice to Washington for conferences with Roosevelt. When, on the second trip, he reached the home of a friend with whom he was to stay, he found an invitation from the President asking him to dine at the White House at eight that evening. Roosevelt, the members of his family, and a gentleman from Colorado were present at the table. After dinner Washington and the President talked at some length about policies involving the South and race relations, and later that night Washington took a train to New York.

The next morning Washington read in the *Tribune* an insignificant report of his visit to the White House. For a day or two nothing happened. Then a Southern correspondent picked up the dispatch, and overnight the affair became a national sensation. Some of the comment was relatively mild, but other Southern editors outdid themselves in an orgy of alarm and denunciation. The Macon *Telegraph* warned that "God set up the barrier between the races. No President of this or any country can break it down." "The mere fact that this nigger Washington accepted the invitation of the President to sit down to dine with him," railed the Memphis *Scimitar*, "is conclusive proof of the utter impossibility of ever doing anything with the nigger, because he (Washington) is certainly the best type of the race we know." The *Commercial Appeal* of the same city attacked the President, saying that Roosevelt had cut himself off socially from the South; that no Southern woman with any self-respect would now accept an invitation to the White House; and that the President would no longer be welcome in Southern homes. A prominent minister declared, "If Roosevelt or any other kind of velt wishes to live with niggers, I can't help it. . . . But he's got no business as President to be guilty of any such

criminal folly. It's an outrage." Below the Mason-Dixon
Line, young Southerners strummed their mandolins and
sang a new popular song:

> Coon, coon, coon,
> Booker Washington is his name;
> Coon, coon, coon,
> Ain't that a measly shame?
> Coon, coon, coon,
> Morning, night, and noon,
> I think I'd class Mr. Roosevelt
> With a coon, coon, coon.

The incident made the white South suspicious of Washington's motives and marked a distinct setback in his popularity. Gradually, however, the storm blew over. His
standing in the North had not, of course, been affected,
nor had his new influence with the President. Washington,
who greatly admired the President's energy, self-reliance,
and capacity for action, considered Roosevelt "the highest
type of all-round man" that he had ever met. T.R. in
return referred to Washington as "the most useful, as
well as the most distinguished, member of his race in the
world, and one of the most useful, as well as the most
distinguished, of American citizens of any race." Throughout Roosevelt's presidency the relationship between the
White House and Tuskegee was very close.

Indeed, from their first interview it was plain that Roosevelt planned to rely on Washington for advice not only
on Negro appointments but on his whole Southern policy.
In general the object of this policy was to make Republicanism respectable in the South by attracting conservatives of both parties. With this in mind Washington recommended to the President in early October, 1901, before

his second White House visit, the appointment of Thomas G. Jones to a federal judgeship in Alabama. Jones was a conservative Democrat who had fought the Populists in the early nineties and had taken a moderate position on Negro suffrage in the Alabama convention of 1901. Though disgruntled to learn that Jones had voted for Bryan in 1896, the President accepted Washington's advice.

In advising the President on appointments, Washington sought not so much to increase the number of colored officeholders as to raise the level of quality among them. Such a policy alarmed a group of Negroes who had been enjoying the patronage of the federal government. Scott, on a visit to the nation's capital, wrote to his chief at Tuskegee, "The colored brethren here are scared. They don't know what to expect and the word has passed, they say, that you are the 'Warwick' so far as they are concerned." Desire for integrity and ability among Negro appointees made Washington feel personally responsible for those he had recommended. On one occasion, learning that the accounts of a Negro officeholder whom he had endorsed were in question, Washington immediately sent Scott to force the man to resign.

Washington also used his influence at the White House to head off "Lily-whitism" in the South, and in return for Roosevelt's co-operation, helped to keep the Negro vote in the Republican column. The Lily-whites were Southern Republicans who tried to build their party in the South by repudiating traditional Republican support for and protection of the Negro, outdoing Southern Democrats in their eagerness for disfranchisement and other discriminatory legislation. Republican toleration of this movement partly stimulated the founding, in 1890, of the Afro-American Council, led by T. Thomas Fortune and a North Carolina Negro educator, J. C. Price. Eventually falling under Washington's influence, the council tried somewhat ineffectively for more than a decade to give the Negro a voice on racial matters of national scope.

The Lily-white movement was anathema to Washington, who gave "his personal pledge to the colored people throughout the country" that it would be "crushed out." When the Lily-whites excluded Negroes from the state Republican conventions of both North Carolina and Alabama in 1902, the Tuskegee head wrote to a friend, "I confess that I thought I knew something of the meanness and rottenness of the average Southern white Republican, but their actions during the last few weeks have taught me that I did not understand them by all odds. . . . Practically all of them are more or less tainted with 'Lily-whitism.' "

Choosing at this point to work by indirection, Washington went to New York and urged a strong countermove upon James S. Clarkson, a long-time friend of the Negro who was influential in the internal affairs of the Republican party. At Washington's request, Clarkson went to the White House and warned the President that unless he went on record against the insurgence of the Lily-whites, he would rapidly lose Negro support. Roosevelt immediately went into action. He called in a group of Negro leaders to reassure them. Then, to demonstrate his good faith, he appointed W. D. Crum, a Negro physician, to a conspicuous federal post and replaced a prominent Lily-white Republican officeholder in Alabama with a Gold Democrat. In addition, to indicate that he was not deserting the

Negroes in the South, he released to the press Washington's letter of the year before recommending the appointment of Judge Jones. To consolidate these gains, Washington soon afterward persuaded the President to put Alabama Republican affairs in the hands of two men entirely acceptable to Tuskegee.

Negroes were delighted with the President's strong stand, for which Clarkson privately gave Washington the entire credit. "But for your coming to New York and impressing me with the situation, the seriousness of which I had not at all suspected," he wrote to Tuskegee, "the revolt against the President would have run into a stampede which it would have taken years, instead of days, to correct and check." Shortly thereafter, with Washington at the helm, the Afro-American Council became an adjunct of the Republican party and commended the President to the "affection and confidence" of the Negro race.

Roosevelt's action against the Lily-whites was an important factor in keeping Negroes loyal to the Republican party in the election of 1904. When T.R. had won, Washington congratulated him with rare effusiveness: "I cannot find words in which to express my feeling," he wrote. "The result shows that the great heart of the American people beats true and is in the direction of fair play for all, regardless of race or color. . . . I shall urge our people everywhere to manifest their gratitude by showing a spirit of meekness and added usefulness."

Though most Negroes were proud of Washington's political influence and prestige, all did not approve. Given the consistent, if often abortive, tradition of Negro protest born in the leaders of slave insurrections and continued in Frederick Douglass, it was inevitable that Washington's leadership should provoke a challenge from those who objected to a policy of moderation; furthermore, if paradoxically, the higher economic and cultural standards to which his work was contributing helped increasingly to nurture the seeds of this opposition.

Moreover, he had consciously alienated the three principal elements among the early, disorganized dissenters: the ministers and the politicians, to whom the race had traditionally looked for leadership, and the intellectuals. As early as the Madison speech of 1884, when he was only twenty-eight and Tuskegee in its infancy, he had openly condemned the "so-called leaders" of the race, who, he declared, "are as a rule ignorant, immoral preachers or selfish politicians." A severely critical article which he wrote for the *Outlook* in 1892 put him on record against the clergy, and for months afterward brought denunciatory resolutions from every Negro church conference or association which assembled.

Washington's equal contempt for most Negro politicians sprang initially from his year at Wayland Seminary. Later, when the nation's capital was full of Negroes hoping for some political plum from the new McKinley administration, he deliberately and sharply advised his race in a Washington speech to spend less time on office seeking and more in some industrial or business enterprise. Such rebukes as this, and his constant deprecation of political office, did not sit well with Negroes in Washington, and when his influence with Roosevelt gave him almost complete power over Negro appointments, the capital became one of the focal points of opposition to the Tuskegee leadership.

Most of the intellectuals, a small group spiritually de-

scended from the Negro abolitionists, never acknowledged
Washington's leadership. In the first place, they looked
upon his emphasis on vocational training as a tacit admission that the Negro was unfit for higher academic
training. Secondly, they charged that his disavowal of political remedies undermined their continuing battle for
civil and political rights. Finally, they resented his near-
universal popularity because he was so obviously not of
themselves.

No one admitted the latter more readily than Washington himself, who did not take pains to conceal his scorn
for the intellectuals. "I have gotten a large part of my education from actual contact with things, rather than
through the medium of books," he said. "I like to deal
with things as far as possible at firsthand in the way that
the carpenter deals with wood, the blacksmith with iron,
and the farmer with the earth." The intellectuals on the
other hand "understand theories but they do not understand things. . . . They know books but they do not know
men. They know a great deal about the slavery contro-
versy, for example, but they know almost nothing about
the Negro. Especially are they ignorant in regard to the
actual needs of the masses of colored people in the South
today."

During the last years of the century the success of the
white South in disfranchising the Negro and the continued violence of lynch mobs strengthened the hands of
men who felt that Washington's protests were far too
mild. The opposition became vocal when two Boston Negroes, Monroe Trotter and George Forbes, began pub-
lishing a newspaper called the *Guardian*. The moving
spirit was Trotter, a Phi Beta Kappa graduate of Harvard

permeated with a burning resentment of the caste system which had relegated him to a status of inferiority. With his unquestioned gift for invective he lashed out at Washington in the pages of the *Guardian* and succeeded in rallying round himself a little knot of intellectuals who shared, more or less, his point of view.

At first Washington refused to take notice of the *Guardian's* outbursts. He did, however, write a conciliatory letter to one of the ablest of the group, William H. Lewis, a Harvard football coach, lawyer, and later Assistant Attorney General under President Taft. Though eventually converted wholeheartedly to the Tuskegee point of view, Lewis at that time considered Washington almost a traitor to the race. Washington's letter, dated October, 1901, revealed his consummate ability in using the soft answer to turn away wrath. "The main point of this letter," he wrote, "is to say I believe that both you and I are going to be in a position in the future to serve the race effectually, and while it is very probable that we shall always differ as to detailed methods of lifting up the race, it seems to me that if we agree in each doing our best to lift it up, the main point will have been gained. . . . I shall be delighted to work in hearty co-operation with you."

The criticism of the Boston group eventually mounted to such an extent that Washington decided to meet the leaders face to face. T. Thomas Fortune, whose reputation as a champion of civil rights enabled him to act as a mediator, arranged a dinner at Young's Hotel in Boston. After the meal was over, Fortune explained that Washington wanted to give those present a chance to voice their criticism and to offer their ideas as to how the interests of the race could best be served. Each of them in turn took the opportunity to denounce Washington's policies and methods. The meeting reached a climax when Lewis plainly told the Tuskegee head to go back South and attend to his work, "leaving to us the matters political affecting the race." Washington's face, as Fortune described it, "was as inscrutable as a wooden Indian's." When all of his opponents had spoken, he rose slowly and completely chilled the meeting with a half hour's even, unimpassioned description of the work at Tuskegee. Only once, when he thanked them for their candor, did he refer to what had gone before.

Such calm by no means prevailed when Washington went to Boston on another occasion to address a meeting in one of the Negro churches. Trotter, Forbes, and another follower had mobilized a group of hecklers who began to hiss when Washington came onto the platform. Refusing to let him proceed, they hurled at him questions about his attitude on civil and political rights. Within moments the place was in an uproar which did not subside until police arrived, ousted the offenders, and hauled Trotter off to jail. Gratified to read in the papers afterward that Trotter had not been let off with mere payment of a fine, Scott wrote to his chief from Tuskegee, "It will be a good thing for all concerned. If we could now have Forbes and the other man removed, not out of malice but simply because they deserve it, I think it will do much to aid the whole general cause."

The demonstration not only earned Trotter a jail sentence but hurt his effort to make headway against the Tuskegee leadership. Newspapers all over the country condemned his tactics and branded him an extremist. Scott sent to Washington, still on his travels, a batch of clippings which he urged him to read: "I think it will be cheering for you to do so, in that evidence is revealed that the sober thought of the people of this entire country is with you and your efforts to uplift this people." From the White House, too, came a note to Washington deploring the attitude of the Boston group. The net result of the incident was to demonstrate Trotter's unsuitability as a leader. He was too extreme and too unstable (he committed suicide in 1934), and, as even his friends admitted, he was so passionate in his cause that he was sometimes unwise and unfair in his attacks.

The Challenge to Washington's Leadership

THE LEADERSHIP which Monroe Trotter could not provide came in the person of William Edward Burghardt Du Bois, a young Atlanta University professor. The product of a background entirely different from Washington's, Du Bois first approved the Tuskegee philosophy, but gradually rejected it as he concluded that Washington's view of society was too limited and his remedy for the Negro's ills insufficient if not positively harmful. As the spokesman for a small but articulate minority of Negroes, Du Bois came to personify a point of view in which protest, in contrast to Washington's tendency to accommodation, was the central element.

Du Bois was born in the western Massachusetts town of Great Barrington in 1868, "with a flood of Negro blood, a strain of French, a bit of Dutch, but, thank God! no 'Anglo-Saxon.'" Great Barrington boasted little wealth, and "Willy" Du Bois did not notice any great disparity between his own station and that of the children with whom he associated. Nor did he meet with prejudice, except in isolated instances, but was, on the contrary, "a center and sometimes the leader of the town gang of boys." Only gradually did he begin to feel himself apart from the rest: "The realization came slowly — although at times there were sudden revelations. Curious enough, however, I always felt myself the superior, not the inferior, and any advantages which they had were, I was sure, quite accidental. I had only to mobilize my dreams — then they would see!"

Graduating from high school with honors at the age of sixteen, he determined to go on to college, and settled fixedly upon Harvard. Influential white men of the town, however, counseled him to go to Fisk, and in 1885, at the age of seventeen, Du Bois boarded the train for the South. Far from submitting to the new experience of segregation and caste with anything like fear, he took a fierce joy in the company of his own race: "A new loyalty and allegiance replaced my Americanism; henceforward I was a Negro." In a surge of race consciousness he replaced his "hitherto egocentric world" with a world centering about his race in America. To this group he transferred his plans: "Through the leadership of men like me and my fellows, we were going to have these enslaved Israelites out of the still-enduring bondage in short order."

Graduating from Fisk in 1888, a year before the first meeting there between Margaret Murray and Booker T. Washington, he reverted to his original desire to attend Harvard. The lack of money and the fact that Harvard would admit him only as a junior were minor obstacles; he "reveled in the keen analysis of William James, Josiah Royce, and young George Santayana," and by 1890 had earned his bachelor's degree. "Commencement came," he later wrote, "and standing before Governor, President, and grave, gowned men, I told them certain astonishing truths, waving my arms and breathing fast. They applauded rapturously, and I walked home on great pink clouds of glory. I asked for a fellowship — and got it. I announced my plan of studying in Germany, and when the Slater Board excused itself, I went at them hammer and tongs. Ex-President Hayes, their chairman, smiled as he surrendered."

In Germany he found a broadening and deepening influence in the teaching of several of the most noted scholars of the time, but study formed only a part of his European education. On foot and by third-class railway he covered central Europe, and in the company of Europeans, where he gained unqualified acceptance, he enjoyed the freedom from discrimination. Two years later, anxious to use his intellectual equipment, he sailed for home. Booker T. Washington, if he had seen Du Bois on the return voyage, would probably never have offered him, as he later did, a position at Tuskegee; for Du Bois was almost a caricature of what Washington despised: a highly educated but penniless man, indulging in the affectation of gloves and cane while traveling in the steerage.

Casting about for a place to teach, Du Bois applied at several Negro institutions, including Tuskegee. In his letter to Washington, which began, "President Washington, Sir!" he offered to teach German, philosophy, natural science, or classics, though "my speciality is history and social science." Finally he accepted a position at Wilberforce College, in Ohio. Taking "a few men and women of first-class intelligence" — and here his theory of education for the best minds was coming to the fore — he worked unceasingly with them, at the same time managing to complete requirements for his doctorate at Harvard, which he received in 1895. But unfortunately, Wilberforce was uninterested in the one field which he considered the most important: sociology. Seeing little chance of changing the situation, he began to look for a more receptive environment.

After a year in Philadelphia, where he made an exhaustive study of life in the predominantly Negro Seventh Ward under the auspices of the University of Pennsylvania, he accepted a position on the faculty of Atlanta University. Here at last was an opportunity for development of his sociological program. At this time he firmly believed that the race problem was "a matter of systematic investigation and intelligent understanding. The world was thinking wrong about race, because it did not know. The ultimate evil was stupidity. The cure for it war knowledge based on scientific investigation." Du Bois embarked on a series of studies desgined to probe every phase of Negro life, feeling as he did that the Negro race in the South offered material for a vast laboratory experiment in social science. Though he was not able to hold consistently to his program, his twenty monographs, published over the next two decades, provided valuable source material in the areas of Negro population, health, morals and manners, education, religion, crime and law enforcement, and the arts.

Soon, however, his experience in Atlanta began to shake his confidence in scientific investigation. Up to that time he had never come to grips with the realities of race prejudice, but in the Georgia city he "became widely acquainted with the real condition" of his people. From "captious criticism" he changed to "cold science; then to hot, indignant defense," holding back "more hardly each day the mounting indignation against injustice and misrepresentation." As he began to realize that the social scientist could not work *in vacuo,* he became increasingly critical of the calm and moderation with which Booker T. Washington met situations "that called — shrieked — for action." At first almost without realizing it, he felt himself swept into the current of active protest against the Washington leadership.

This change came gradually. At the time of the Atlanta speech, Du Bois by no means sided with the small minority of critics. As he wrote later, "I was not overcritical of Booker T. Washington. I regarded his Atlanta speech as a statesmanlike effort to reach understanding with the white South. I hoped the South would respond with equal generosity and thus the nation would come to understanding for both races." Indeed, early in January, 1896, when he was anxious to leave Wilberforce, Du Bois wrote to ask Washington's help in finding a new position, concluding the letter, "I trust your work is progressing as it deserves to." Three months later, after Washington had suggested the possibility of an opening at Tuskegee, Du Bois wrote again to tell him of the Philadelphia project. Perhaps after the year in Philadelphia he would be needed at Tuskegee. "At any case," Du Bois said, "I am willing and eager to entertain any proposition for giving my services to your school."

These cordial relations continued for some years. In the spring of 1899, Du Bois accepted Washington's invitation to read an original story at a meeting in behalf of Tuskegee at the Hollis Street Theater in Boston. Paul Laurence Dunbar, the Negro poet, appeared on the same program, which gave the two young Negroes their first opportunity for public recognition in Boston. In addition, Du Bois attended several of the annual Tuskegee Conferences, and on at least one other occasion again discussed with Washington the possibility of joining the Tuskegee faculty. By early 1903, however, Du Bois was definitely moving toward the opposition. A letter he wrote at that time inviting Washington to the Atlanta University Conference, which was trying to do for urban Negroes what the Tuskegee Conference was doing for their rural brethren, struck a sharp note not found in their previous correspondence. Emphasizing that he had "sought in every way to minimize the breach between colleges and industrial schools," and had "in all possible ways tried to co-operate with Tuskegee in its work," Du Bois pointedly added, "I have not been so successful in getting you to co-operate with ours, altho' this is of course due to the fact that you are a busy man."

Du Bois voiced his first public criticism of Washington in *The Souls of Black Folk,* a series of essays published in 1903 and permeated with his growing resentment. What caught the public eye was a section entitled, "Of Mr. Booker T. Washington and Others," which, though it recognized the Tuskegee educator's achievements, unmistakably took him to task on a number of counts. Washington's educational program, declared Du Bois, was "unnecessarily narrow," and had developed into a "gospel of Work and Money to such an extent as apparently almost completely to overshadow the higher aims of life." His failure to see that no educational system could exist "on any other basis than that of the well-equipped college or university," and his corresponding overemphasis on industrial training, Du Bois continued, was stunting the growth of Negro higher education and destroying the opportunity for developing the best minds of the race.

In the realm of civil rights Washington had, it was true, spoken against disfranchisement and lynching. But his protest was far too mild, and his voluntary surrender of full citizenship had "without a shadow of a doubt" aided the white man's effort to take away the Negro's ballot and assign him to "a distinct status of civil inferiority." "We have no right to sit silently by," Du Bois asserted, "while the inevitable seeds are sown for a harvest of disaster to our children, black and white."

Furthermore, Washington's emphasis on self-help had "tended to make the whites, North and South, shift the burden of the Negro problem to the Negro's shoulders and stand aside as critical and rather pessimistic spectators." It was not a problem for one race or for one region, as Washington tended to think, but a problem for the nation. The Negro could not hope for success "unless his striving be not simply seconded, but rather aroused and encouraged, by the initiative of the richer and wiser environing group."

Finally, Du Bois warned of a group of "educated and thoughtful" Negroes who were alarmed by some of Washington's theories and who had never accepted wholeheartedly his leadership, thrust upon them as it had been by "outer pressure." Their criticism had been largely hushed by public opinion, but they now felt "in conscience bound" to ask of the nation three things: the right to vote, civic equality, and the education of youth according to ability. So far as Washington preached thrift, patience, and industrial training for the masses, they would support him. "But," Du Bois concluded, "so far as Mr. Washington apoligizes for injustice, North or South, does not rightly value the privilege and duty of voting, belittles the emasculating effects of caste distinctions, and opposes the higher training and ambition of our brighter minds — so far as he, the South, or the Nation, does this — we must unceasingly and firmly oppose them."

The Souls of Black Folk received favorable notice from many critics, particularly as to its literary merit. But Washington's prestige was too great to be damaged by its criticism, and journals like the *Nation,* admitting that the essay should be soberly considered at Tuskegee, chided Du Bois for overstatement. Nevertheless, it served notice that the ranks of the opposition were forming and that a new personality had arisen to provide the leadership.

During the last twelve years of his life, from 1903 to 1915, Washington was pursued relentlessly by his self-appointed gadfly, Du Bois. Soon departing from the measured, restrained tones of *The Souls of Black Folk,* Du Bois elaborated his attack to take issue with Washington on almost every point of his program. This is not to say that the public viewed them as champions of opposing armies; most laymen had never heard of Du Bois, who undoubtedly had delusions of grandeur when he pictured himself after 1905 as "the leader of a great wing of people fighting against another and greater wing." But within the narrow circle of Negroes anxious to have a part in determining race leadership and program, the struggle between Washington and Du Bois was of real significance.

Except for a common dedication to the cause of race advancement, the personalities of the two men differed as widely as their ideas. Washington was a practical realist, interested primarily in attaining tangible goals; Du Bois was a romantic, willing and eager to fight for principle even if the battle cost him his life. In contrast to Du Bois's poetic temperament, Washington's was simple, direct, prosaic. Though Du Bois as an intellectual liked to deal with ideas, while Washington preferred men and things, Du Bois was by far the more emotional. Washington was first and last an American, Du Bois first and last a Negro. Washington possessed a genuine humility and an ability to identify himself with the common man; Du Bois was imperious, egocentric, aloof. To Du Bois, Washington's faith in man and God was somewhat naïve.

In his critique of the Tuskegee philosophy, Du Bois denied the hypothesis on which Washington's program rested: the necessity of co-operation with the white South. He could not agree that there was a solidarity of interest between the Southern Negro and the Southern white man which made the race problem one to be solved from within. The price for co-operation and support, according to Du Bois, was too high: "Today the young Negro of the South who would succeed cannot be frank and outspoken. . . . He must flatter and be pleasant, endure petty insults with a smile, shut his eyes to wrong. . . . His real thoughts, his real aspirations, must be guarded in whispers." Even had he rationally accepted Washington's premise, Du Bois would have found it hard to follow him emotionally; for to Du Bois the white man was an enemy rather than a friend.

Washington, who had begun with a distinct envy of the dominant race, had been much impressed by the attitude of General Armstrong. "I never heard him speak . . . a single bitter word against the white man in the

South," Washington testified. "From his example in this respect I learned the lesson that great men cultivate love, and that only little men cherish a spirit of hatred." Finding "that hating the white man did not do him any harm, and it certainly was narrowing up my soul and making me a good bit less of a human being," Washington said, "I will quit hating the white man." He was then able to believe that "if the black man in the South has a friend in his white neighbor, and a still larger number of friends in his own community, he has a protection and a guarantee of his rights that will be more potent and more lasting than any our Federal Congress or any outside power can confer."

To Du Bois such a belief was incredible, and every injustice he encountered made it seem more so. The Atlanta race riot of 1906 clearly demonstrated the difference in their attitudes. On that occasion, as the result of sensational press reports of four alleged attempts at rape, ill feeling between Negroes and whites flamed into active warfare which paralyzed the city for three days. Business houses, their show windows smashed, hastily closed their doors; factory machinery ground to a stop; wrecked street-cars lay helpless on their sides. Property damage reached an alarming total, but the greatest loss was in human life: more than one hundred persons, the majority of them Negroes, were killed or wounded.

Washington, in New England at the time of the riot, canceled his engagements and went immediately to Atlanta. Urging Negroes not to make "the fatal mistake of attempting to retaliate" but to "rely upon the efforts of the proper authorities to bring order and security out of confusion," he conferred with city authorities and organized a meeting of ten leading citizens of each race to discuss a course of action. With the situation under control, this body established a permanent interracial committee to work for co-operation between whites and Negroes and thereby to avoid future outbreaks. Publicly Washington advised his race to remember that "while there is disorder in one community, there is peace and harmony in thousands of others." After a second visit to Atlanta several months later, Washington reported a "general spirit of repentance and sorrow among the white people," and observed that "incendiary speeches" would now do more harm than good.

Du Bois, also out of the city when the riot began, hurried homeward. After it was over, he wrote an account of the tragedy for the *World Today* in which he pled fervently for the protection of the Negro by a more efficient police system, better schools, the return of the ballot, and federal legislation. But the undercurrent of deep protest in this relatively restrained appeal did not express his real feelings nearly so well as the fiercely bitter "Litany of Atlanta," which he composed on the train during the height of the rioting. Such events as the Atlanta riot nourished his malevolence, until finally he burst out in an essay entitled, "The Souls of White Folk," with:

> The white world's vermin and filth:
> All the dirt of London,
> All the scum of New York;
> Valiant spoilers of women
> And conquerors of unarmed men . . .
> Bearing the white man's burden
> Of liquor and lust and lies.
> I hate them, Oh!
> I hate them well,

I hate them, Christ!
As I hate hell.

Since he could not believe that the average Southern white man had any desire to help the Negro, Du Bois could see no future in the South for the ambitious young people of his race. Directly contradicting Washington's counsel, Du Bois urged them to go North for freedom and advancement. A city dweller by temperament, he encouraged the urban migration at every turn, believing that the country represented "oppression and serfdom," while the city represented opportunity.

Since both were educators, their divergence in educational philosophy became the focal point of their most widely publicized disagreement. To Du Bois, an intellectual who had no doubt that the really important things of life lay in the realm of the mind, Washington's emphasis on bank accounts and ownership of property was abhorrent. Deploring the fact that "for every social ill the panacea of wealth has been urged," he insisted that "the object of all true education is not to make men carpenters, it is to make carpenters men." He hooted at the "Tuskegee Idea" that education should begin at the bottom and expand upward. "Was there ever," he asked, "a nation on God's fair earth civilized from the bottom upward? Never; it is, ever was, and ever will be from the top downward that culture filters."

Therefore he championed the cause of higher education for the best Negro minds at institutions like Atlanta, Fisk, and Howard, setting forth the doctrine of the "Talented Tenth," a term which became the trade-mark of his educational philosophy: "The Talented Tenth of the Negro race must be made leaders of thought and missionaries of culture among their people. No others can do this work and Negro colleges must train men for it. The Negro race, like all other races, is going to be saved by its exceptional men."

Washington vigorously denied that he opposed the higher training and ambition of the brighter minds of the race. "I would not by any means have it understood," he insisted, "that I would limit or circumscribe the mental development of the Negro student." Recalling the many industrial schools in Germany, the "home" of scholarship, he made plain his opposition to the "ill-advised" notion that industrial education meant class education to which the Negro should be confined. Industrial education "should be given in a large measure to any race, regardless of color, which is in the same stage of development as the Negro," he maintained. But there was obviously "a place and an increasing need for the Negro college as well as the industrial institution, and the two classes of schools should, and as a matter of fact do, co-operate in the common purpose of elevating the masses." As evidence of his sincerity he called attention to the fact that many members of his faculty had come from liberal-arts colleges rather than industrial schools of the Tuskegee variety.

Du Bois hastened to make clear that he also favored a balanced educational program. He welcomed industrial schools at the ratio of ten to one, he declared, provided a few institutions of high standing were maintained to give his "Talented Tenth" that "knowledge of the forces of civilization that make for survival, ability to organize and guide those forces, and realization of the true meaning of those broader ideals of human betterment which may in time bring heaven and earth a little nearer."

His open break with Washington pushed Du Bois toward an alliance with Trotter, whom he had known slightly at Harvard. Several months after *The Souls of Black Folk* appeared, Du Bois went to Boston on Trotter's invitation, only to learn as he got off the train that his host had just been arrested for breaking up Washington's meeting at Zion Church. Since Du Bois had recently been lecturing at Tuskegee summer school despite his criticism of Washington, he was at first irritated at being placed in an awkward position, but he soon decided that Trotter had been unjustly treated and went over to his defense.

In the summer of 1905, feeling that only organized protest could make an effective dent in the Washington armor, Du Bois issued a call to a number of Negroes, including Trotter, to meet at Niagara Falls. Twenty-nine men responded. Since the American hotels would not admit them, they met on the Canadian side, where they dedicated themselves to work unceasingly for the abolition of all caste distinctions based on race and color, and served notice to the world through the "Garrison pledge of the Niagara Movement" that they too would be "as harsh as truth and as uncompromising as justice," and that they too would be heard.

With Du Bois as the dominant force, the group held two more meetings, the next in 1906 at Harpers Ferry, Virginia, where, in their leader's words, they "made pilgrimage at dawn barefooted to the scene of Brown's martyrdom" and "talked some of the plainest English that has been given voice to by black men of America." The Niagara Movement, however, was a feeble effort, hampered as it was by a lack of funds and influential white friends. It had a melodramatic quality, characteristic of Du Bois in his early years, which kept many from taking it seriously; the thought of a group of men marching barefooted at dawn around the fort at Harpers Ferry, singing "John Brown's Body" as they went, bordered on the burlesque. Nevertheless, the Niagara Movement did furnish the nucleus of Negro membership in the National Association for the Advancement of Colored People which followed in 1910, and for five years its members kept alive the challenge to Washington's leadership. One of Washington's friends observed just after the initial meeting at Niagara Falls, "Du Bois has not the make-up of a popular leader, but as the official head of the concentrated jealousy of the country, he can carry on a guerrilla-like warfare that is decidedly uncomfortable."

Believing that "extremes of utterance or action" seriously damaged the Negro's efforts, Washington heartily disapproved of the Niagara group's tactics despite their repeated assurance that the movement had "no purpose to oppose or in any way embarrass" him. He had an open contempt for them as "a class of colored people who make a business of keeping the troubles, the wrongs, and the hardships of the Negro race before the public." Such people, he said, "think that the whole salvation of the race is to be worked out by a series of indignation meetings," which they organized "every time something does not go to suit them." His usual practice was to ignore attacks upon him and his leadership; as he wrote to a friend in 1903, "Silence will hurt Trotter and his crowd worse than anything else."

His disposition was also to pay no attention to the Niagara Movement. As Scott confided to a friend, "If we consistently refuse to take the slightest notice of them

. . . the whole thing will die a-borning." That this treatment did not succeed is indicated by a second letter shortly afterward advising "that our friends might just as well turn in now and hammer the Niagara Movement for all that they can." Though he continued to ignore the movement publicly, Washington was stung by what he considered unfair attacks. He did not often reveal his feelings, but in September, 1905, he expressed himself in plain language to Whitefield McKinlay: "I am very anxious," he wrote, "to know what effect, if any, the vile work which Trotter, Du Bois, and that gang have been doing lately in conjunction with the most filthy newspapers in the South has had upon the colored people in Washington." Denouncing them as "scoundrels" for paying lip service to individual liberty and "manhood rights" while "missing no opportunity to join the vile element in the South in condemnation of me for exercising those same rights outside of the South in the way I have always done," Washington concluded that "nothing seems to be beyond them."

As the attacks continued and the influence of the *Guardian*, which had become the principal voice of the Niagara Movement, seemed to be spreading, Washington decided to rehabilitate the Afro-American Council. Together with Bishop Alexander Walters of New York, at that time friendly to him, he resurrected the old organization in 1906 to counteract the harsh protest of the Niagara group with more moderate pronouncements. However, the Chicago *Conservator*, one of the few Negro newspapers sympathetic toward the opposition, observed that the council would not have met "had there been no Niagara Movement to disturb the sweet balance of the man whose tools stole the Afro-American Council from the Negro race."

Despite occasional strong language in letters to friends, Washington had a remarkable capacity for practicing privately the moderation and calm he preached in public. He did not harbor grudges. At times, when Du Bois had struck home with particularly telling effect, Washington could refer to him as a "scoundrel," as he did in the letter of 1905 to McKinlay. On the other hand, he could write to a friend in 1909 that "Dr. Du Bois has really a very fine and sensible article in the May *World's Work*," and suggest having reprints made for distribution. Then he added in amused tolerance that he did not know how Du Bois would like it, for "Du Bois is such a big dunce that one never knows how to take him. . . . I have an idea that he is learning a little sense but I am not sure of this." Again, when a representative of the Anti-Slavery and Aborigines Protection Society, which had been asked to facilitate Du Bois's visit to England in 1911, wrote to Tuskegee for advice, Washington spoke "most highly" of Du Bois's "excellent work" and counseled the society to do what it could to assist him.

With rare exceptions, Washington was also open and straightforward in his personal relationships, and remained on cordial terms with many who disagreed with him; among these were such men as the Negro writer Charles W. Chesnutt and the president of Atlanta University, John Hope. Nothing so annoyed him, however, as what he considered underhanded blows. As he wrote of one Negro minister, "If he wanted to attack me he had an opportunity during the three days we were together face to face in a manly straightforward way, but he was too big a coward for that, but waited until he got an opportunity to do so behind my back." He could also be very humble. To a critic who charged that press releases from Tuskegee were giving Washington too much personal publicity, he admitted that in keeping the school before the public, his secretary had perhaps "sent out too much matter to the colored papers in laudation of myself," and promised to see "that he is more careful in the future."

As Du Bois admitted, some of the criticism of Washington stemmed from "mere envy" and from "the disappointment of displaced demagogues and the spite of narrow minds." Even Du Bois's own attacks occasionally showed a distinctly personal element. But Washington could afford to be magnanimous; the fact that the Anti-Slavery Society, a British organization, should have felt it necessary to ask his advice before extending a welcome to Du Bois demonstrated how completely Washington dominated the scene. It was this very domination which the opposition group so resented. Their differences with Washington sprang from a sincere and significant disagreement on the approach to advancement for the Negro, but mainly they feared that the ascendancy of the "Tuskegee Machine," as Du Bois called it, had given Washington a power over Negro affairs which should not be vested in any individual.

X

Benevolent Despot

THAT WASHINGTON'S influence permeated the entire American Negro community cannot be doubted. According to his critics, he controlled the outlets of Northern philanthropy to such an extent that little or no money went to liberal-arts institutions, dominated the Negro press so completely as to make any disagreement with his views almost impossible, and carried such weight in federal appointments of Negroes that his withholding of the scepter of approval was fatal. When, in 1909, influential white people joined the small nucleus within the Negro race who objected to Washington's policies and leadership, the National Association for the Advancement of Colored People emerged to hold up the standard for the opposing view.

Each of the opposition charges contained more than a little truth. Washington unquestionably had a great deal to say about the allocation of large sums from Northern foundations and from individual philanthropists. "I have kept up pretty closely with all these schools during the year," he wrote of a list he had been asked to review, "and I have also looked carefully through the list of new schools that have made application to Mr. Schiff; some of them are worthy and some of them unworthy — I mean the new ones. You will notice that I have made only one or two changes as compared with last year." On another occasion he wrote that he did not believe a certain university "would come in the class of schools which Mr. Rosenwald is desirous of helping at this time." Andrew Carnegie regularly consulted Washington about institutions which appealed to him for funds and, like others, sought his advice on white as well as Negro colleges.

In his control of the Negro press, benevolent though it may have been, Washington laid himself open to real criticism. He could say truthfully in 1911 that with the exception of "about three" the two hundred Negro newspapers had stood loyally by him in all his plans and policies; but in some instances they had stood by him for reasons that were not apparent to the public. Especially after Scott's arrival, Washington had an active public-relations force which distributed reams of material favorable to the Tuskegee leadership. Though much of this concerned genuinely newsworthy events, much also went out in the form of editorials which bore no indication of their origin when they eventually appeared in print. Often Washington used such editorials and "letters to the editor" to protest more vehemently against discrimination than he cared to do in public, but he and his staff also used them to counteract unfavorable publicity. In some cases, the printing of such material was encouraged by occasional "contributions" to Negro editors.

On at least one occasion he resorted to pressure to keep an editor in line. In 1905 Scott wrote to Bishop John C. Dancy of the A. M. E. Zion Church that the young editor of the *Star of Zion*, official organ of the church, was being "used" by a clique hostile to the Tuskegee philosophy. Washington had never objected to legitimate opposition, Scott told the bishop, but did object to a complete misrepresentation of the sentiment of the race. In addition, Scott reminded Dancy rather pointedly of Washington's friendship (Dancy had been appointed to a federal office on Washington's endorsement) and of his efforts to obtain a library for one of the A. M. E. Zion colleges. Dancy replied immediately that he would set the offending editor straight, and shortly thereafter called Washington's attention to a very favorable article in the current issue of the *Star of Zion.*

After the beginning of the Niagara Movement, Washington took even more positive steps to guarantee a favorable press. For some time Scott had been sending out material through R. W. Thompson, who operated a news agency in Indiana which served, according to its letterhead, "all leading colored journals in America." In October, 1905, Thompson suggested that "for strategic purposes" he would like to move his business to the nation's capital, where he could better serve Tuskegee, the government department in which he had a minor appointment, and himself. Washington approved and used his influence to have Thompson transferred. With Thompson directly obligated to him, Washington had an agent in the nation's capital through whom he could easily influence most of the prominent Negro papers.

Of equal consequence was Washington's secret ownership of the New York *Age,* which, as he said, was "the strongest and most widely circulated Negro paper in the country . . . one of the very few that deserve the name of being national." As early as 1904, Washington had writ-

ten to Fortune, its editor and part owner, offering ob-
liquely to buy the *Age* from him and his partner, J. B.
Peterson, with the stipulation that they might continue
their connection with the paper on a salary basis. This
letter suggested that the scope of the *Age* could be broadened to make it a national weekly which could "control
in a very large degree the whole Negro situation."

Nothing came of this early offer. But in the autumn of
1905, fearing that the *Age* might fall into the hands of
the opposition, Washington again approached Fortune.
They agreed that an editor named Fred Moore, acting on
Washington's behalf, should buy Fortune's interest for
$7000 and take over the direction of the paper. Peterson,
who handled the business management of the *Age,* was to
know nothing of the source of Moore's funds, and even
Scott never knew where Washington got the money to
make the purchase. The debt to Fortune was paid off in
installments over a period of several years after the sale in
1906.

After the purchase, Washington gave to the *Age* the
same kind of personal attention he gave to anything which
interested him. Insistent that the paper maintain high
standards, he continually jogged Moore about his methods, reprimanding him for marking items, "Special to the
Age," when they had appeared first in other papers, for
dating letters to the editor improperly, for letting others
get ahead of him — even for failing to keep the office
clean. Moore regularly received letters from Tuskegee like
one which read, "Dear Mr. Moore: Will you kindly see
that the enclosed editorials are published? Yours truly,
Booker T. Washington." Washington also asked for
monthly financial statements and gave definite orders, ad-

visory in form but mandatory in tone, as to what should and should not be included in the *Age's* columns.

After rigidly controlling the paper's policies for five years, Washington decided in 1910 to "get rid of all relations with the publication." That there were unsavory aspects about the arrangement is shown by a letter written to Scott by an accountant whom Washington had employed to examine the financial operations of the paper in 1909. It was against his judgment, the accountant reported, not to be candid with Mr. Peterson "as to the real ownership of the majority interest," for Moore had lied to Peterson, and the misrepresentation was "apt to engender bad blood in the end." Of course, the letter concluded, "you and Mr. Washington may consider it dangerous to let Mr. Peterson know the facts; if so, I have nothing further to say."

The ownership of the *Age* had led Washington into a direct misrepresentation, which was not characteristic of him. When, in 1907, relations between Fortune and Tuskegee cooled, the former editor began to tell friends privately about the sale of the *Age*. The rumor got out, and Washington was forced either to admit control of the paper, which he did not feel he could afford to do, or deny it. In a letter to the editor of the *Western Opinion,* a Negro newspaper in Chicago, he did the latter. "I do not own or control a single newspaper or other publication in America," he insisted. "I have refrained from investing money in newspaper property for the reason that any man holding a public position before the world as I do ought not to try to influence newspapers in a financial matter."

By 1911 Moore had taken over full responsibility for the *Age,* writing in November of that year that no one controlled him or the policy of the paper. However, Scott still retained some stock, and Tuskegee's "friendship" for the *Age,* as Scott put it, remained strong. As late as 1915, Washington was still giving Moore advice on his editorial policies.

Though he tried to play down his political influence, denying as "wholly without foundation" the charge that he distributed patronage for the President, Washington did exercise the near-absolute control over Negro political affairs which Du Bois attributed to him. Roosevelt, who demonstrated his friendship for Washington by visiting Tuskegee in 1905, continued to ask his advice on every Negro appointment, a policy which Taft also followed. As Scott admitted with pride after Washington's death, "During the administrations of both President Roosevelt and Taft hardly an office of consequence was conferred upon a Negro without first consulting Mr. Washington."

Washington not only advised Roosevelt and Taft on appointments, but also helped them phrase statements of public policy in such a way as to elicit maximum approval (or, in some cases, to cause the least objection) from the Negro public. Of one Roosevelt speech which he altered substantially he wrote Fortune, "I do not mind saying to you in confidence that if the speech had been delivered as it was first prepared, it would not have given any great satisfaction to our people." In this capacity Washington was of particular assistance to Taft, whose statements concerning the Negro he carefully screened during the campaign for the Presidential nomination in 1908. Washington also helped draft the "Negro part" of Taft's acceptance speech. The grateful President-elect sent word after the election that he wished to consult Washington "fully and freely on all racial matters" during his administration.

There was a curious ambivalence in Washington's Republicanism. Time and again he warned the Negro not to put all his eggs blindly in the Republican basket, but in every major election, with an allegiance which would have done justice to the most loyal ward heeler, he threw all his influence toward maintaining the Negro's traditional political alignment. Roosevelt's ready co-operation in Washington's campaign against the Lily-whites made this fairly easy in the election of 1904, but the task became progressively more difficult because of T.R.'s and Taft's inconsistent racial policies.

Roosevelt first gave Negroes pause when, at the beginning of his second term, he set out in earnest to build support among Southern whites by praising Robert E. Lee and presenting flowers to Stonewall Jackson's widow during an extensive good-will tour of the South. Politically conscious Negroes also had misgivings about the Roosevelt-Washington emphasis on quality rather than quantity in Negro appointments, a policy which many considered better in theory than in practice. But the event which crystallized anti-Roosevelt sentiment among Negroes was his handling of the Brownsville case involving Negro troops in 1906.

In August of that year soldiers of the Twenty-fifth Infantry Regiment, a Negro unit stationed at Brownsville, Texas, became involved in an altercation with whites of the town which developed into a full-blown race riot. One man was killed and several others were seriously wounded as the troops allegedly "shot up the town." When the riot was over, the War Department, then under the direction of Secretary Taft, launched an exhaustive investigation to ferret out the guilty. Though they freely testified of persecution by the whites of Brownsville, the soldiers refused to incriminate any of their fellows. Incensed, the President threatened to discharge every man in the three companies involved, and when questioning of every man in the group failed to produce any results, he carried out his threat.

In this instance, a personal visit by Washington to the White House could do nothing to alter the decision, for public sentiment was running high, and the New York *Times* reported a widespread feeling at the War Department that Roosevelt had contributed to the incident by social recognition of the Negro. The majority of white people, and especially Southern whites, supported the President, but Negroes of all stations and political leanings bitterly resented his action. Though the press revealed Washington's unsuccessful intercession with Roosevelt, Niagara Movement papers seized the opportunity to condemn Washington for having concurred in the White House move.

Because he was Roosevelt's personal choice and because as Secretary of War he shouldered part of the responsibility for the Brownsville incident, Taft's nomination by the Republican party in 1908 did not evoke enthusiasm among Negroes. To make matters worse, Roosevelt and Taft agreed upon an ex-Confederate soldier, Luke Wright, to head the War Department as Taft's successor. Despite his warning to Taft that this appointment would further alienate Negroes from the party, Washington felt that since the Democratic party was actively hostile to the colored race, the Negro had all to lose and nothing to gain by deserting the Republicans, whatever their shortcomings.

Consequently, Washington worked closely with the

chairman of the Republican National Committee during the campaign to mitigate Negro opposition to the Republican ticket. When R. W. Thompson told him that Negro editors would have to be given financial inducements to support Taft, Washington obtained from the national committee funds which were doled out to influential Negro papers through Thompson's News Bureau. In addition, Washington used his widespread influence with prominent men of the race, for many of whom he had obtained political favors. When Taft won, Thompson wrote enthusiastically to Scott that Washington's leadership was now unquestionable, and that the "Washington Cabinet," constructed "after careful scrutiny," was "the finest 'machine' ever gotten together by a Negro in the history of the world."

Even Washington's "machine" could not check the revolt against Taft which had developed among Negroes by 1912. In a bid for Southern favor even more pronounced than Roosevelt's, the President also made a tour of the South, where he seemed to condone disfranchisement and to accept Southern hypotheses about the Negro. When he suited action to words by reducing the number of Negro appointees, leaders of the race in all sections turned against him. By 1910 Thompson reported that Negroes in Washington were growing restive under the "narrow practices" of Tuskegee's friends, who were accused of having formed a "closed corporation" to perpetuate themselves in office. From a lifelong friend in Mississippi came a report that Negro leaders there, most of whom had not really favored Taft's nomination in 1908, were now completely disillusioned. When Taft refused to heed a plea from Tuskegee not to remove John C. Dancy from his federal post in

1910, Washington admitted that he shared the general dissatisfaction with the President. "I think you will agree with me," he remarked to a friend, "that this administration has been more successful in turning people out than it has been in putting them in."

Distaste for the President served only to complicate the Negro's choice in the election of 1912. Roosevelt's attempt to enlist Southern support for the Progressive party led him to measures which, added to the memories of Brownsville, made him no more acceptable than Taft, and Wilson was not only a Democrat, but a Southerner by birth. Faced with a choice of evils, Washington remained with Taft and again helped him with his acceptance speech. Washington did not, however, allow himself to become deeply involved in the election and wrote to an influential Negro friend, "You are free, as you know, without any word from me, to act in any way that your own judgment and conscience dictates." His only real effort during the campaign was to head off a resurgence of the Lily-white movement in some of the Southern states.

Taft's defeat meant the end of Washington's close association with the White House. Though his relations with Wilson, whom he knew even before the election, were cordial enough, Washington's complete identification with the Republican party for more than fifteen years meant that he could not expect to become an intimate adviser to a Democratic administration.

President Wilson's executive order establishing segregated facilities for colored federal employees, together with the flood of discriminatory legislation introduced in the first Democratic Congress, made Negroes suspect that the New Freedom offered them little that was new and little that was freedom. But regardless of this, the hopes that Theodore Roosevelt's friendship had raised among Negroes at the beginning of the new century had faded some time before. Even under Roosevelt and Taft, lynchings had continued at the rate of about one hundred a year, and the influx of Southern Negroes into Northern cities caused a sharp increase in urban race riots. Southern states added new disfranchising devices, while Baltimore's enactment of residential segregation began a movement which quickly spread to other towns and cities.

The bloody race riot of August, 1908, in Lincoln's own home of Springfield, Illinois, served as the catalyst for the rising indignation against such conditions. After a visit to Springfield, the socialist William English Walling wrote an article for the *Independent* which warned that if the Negro were not immediately given full political and social equality, "Vardaman and Tillman will soon have transferred the Race War to the North." Together with Mary White Ovington, a New York social worker, Dr. Henry Moskowitz, and Oswald Garrison Villard, grandson of William Lloyd Garrison and editor of the New York *Evening Post,* Walling called for "all believers in democracy" to meet on Lincoln's birthday, 1909, for "the renewal of the struggle for civil and political liberty." Noting the obvious similarity of the Niagara Movement's aims, they invited Du Bois and his followers to meet with them.

The group which assembled in New York included Moorfield Storey, at one time secretary to Charles Sumner and later president of the American Bar Association, Jane Addams, John Dewey, William Dean Howells, Rabbi Stephen S. Wise, Bishop Alexander Walters, Mary White Ovington, Villard, Walling, Du Bois, and others. Washington was conspicuously absent. An intense opposition to conciliation and compromise vied with considerable uncertainty as to desirable practical steps, and many Negro delegates could not conquer their suspicion of the motives of the whites. Trotter withdrew, and one Negro woman leaped to her feet and cried in an impassioned voice, "They are betraying us again — these white friends of ours!"

Despite its difficulties, the conference finally passed by a large majority a platform almost identical with that of the Niagara Movement, demanding strict enforcement of the Constitution with regard to civil rights, equal education for all, and universal enfranchisement. It also approved Villard's suggestion that a committee of forty work out plans for a continuing national organization; the next year the National Association for the Advancement of Colored People was born. Moorfield Storey became its first president, and Du Bois, the only Negro among its executive officers, left Atlanta to become director of the Department of Research and editor of the official magazine, the *Crisis*.

Editorship of the *Crisis* gave Du Bois a weapon with which to attack the "Tuskegee machine" and its policy of moderation. "Is it not time to strike back when we are struck?" he asked his race in an article charging that increasing Negro disabilities were the product of ill-advised counsel from Tuskegee. "Is it not time to hold up our heads and clench our teeth and swear by the Eternal God we will NOT be slaves, and that no aider, abetter and teacher of slavery in any shape or guise can no [*sic*] longer lead us?" Aiming one barb after another at Washington and his followers, Du Bois made clear to his readers that the *Crisis* existed not for entertainment but for "the sole object of arousing their fighting blood."

Washington was naturally interested in the NAACP, and friends in New York kept him informed of its activities. In keeping with his usual practice, he said little or nothing about the organization in public, confiding privately to a friend that all Du Bois and his Negro followers wanted was "free advertising." Still, Washington did not believe in leaving the field to the opposition. As he wrote to Fred Moore of the *Age* a month after the first issue of the *Crisis* appeared, "We must not stand back and let the other fellows do all the fighting. . . . We must go in and show them we are not afraid to battle for our side." When the *Crisis* was claiming a circulation of twelve thousand copies per month, he warned Moore that the *Age* would "have to get to hustling in order to maintain its influence and predominance."

More "constructive" in its approach than the NAACP, and therefore more appealing to Washington, was the National Urban League, founded in 1911 to assist in broadening economic opportunities for Negroes. Growing out of the Committee for Improving Industrial Conditions of Negroes in New York and the National League for the Protection of Colored Women, the Urban League undertook to solve the many new and perplexing problems posed by the urban migration of Negroes. It met the new arrivals, helped them find lodging, offered advice on city living, and, most important, did much to bring employees and employers together. At the same time it was training social workers for leadership in the growing Negro communities.

Washington's active support of the Urban League contrasted sharply with his relationship with the NAACP during the last years of his life. The first open clash came as a result of his speech to the Anti-Slavery and Aborigines Society in London during the autumn of 1910. Washington had gone to Europe for a three months' vacation at the insistence of his board of trustees, but only on the condition that he might spend the time studying the life of those in Europe whose economic, political, and social status most nearly paralleled that of his own race in America. Before he sailed, he resolved not to enter a single palace, museum, gallery, or cathedral, for, as he explained, "I find markets more instructive than museums." The past did not interest him; he preferred "the new, the unfinished, and the problematic."

Robert E. Park of Boston, a well-informed student of European conditions who had arranged Washington's itinerary, traveled with him. In Denmark, Germany, Austria-Hungary, and Italy Washington dictated notes of his impressions, which Park later fashioned for him into a book entitled, *The Man Farthest Down*. In the book Washington concluded that despite obvious handicaps, the Negro was better off than the "man farthest down" in Europe, enjoyed better living conditions, more economic opportunity, better educational facilities, even more political freedom than such Europeans as the Hungarian peasant and the Sicilian miner.

This conclusion colored Washington's address before the Anti-Slavery Society when he reached England on his way home. To the indignation of the NAACP, he emphasized the progress of American Negroes since emancipation and played down their difficulties. A denunciatory circular issued by one member of the new organization immediately after the address stung Washington; he wrote Villard that such attacks did not accord with the purpose of the NAACP as Villard had described it. "When there is so much that is needed to be done," he observed, "in the way of punishing those who are guilty of lynching, of peonage, and seeing that the Negro gets an equitable share of the school fund, and that the law relating to the ballot is enforced in regard to black men and white men, it is difficult to see how people can throw away their time and strength in stirring up strife within the race."

During the spring of 1911, however, Washington and Villard tried to arrive at a basis of mutual co-operation. "I am convinced," Washington wrote, "that the time has come when we should lay aside personal differences and personal bickerings." In addition to arranging for an exchange of fraternal delegates by the NAACP and the Business League, Washington promised to use his influence in toning down criticism of the NAACP in the Negro press provided the NAACP would act in a similar spirit.

This move toward conciliation received further impetus from an incident in March, 1911, which brought Washington genuine sympathy even from his enemies. One Sunday in New York he went into the foyer of an apartment house looking for the apartment of a friend. Uncertain about the door, he was stopping to examine the numbers when a man named Ulrich burst out, choked him, struck him with his fists, and hit him with a stick as they fought their way outside. Ulrich later alleged that Washington had peered under the shade and through the keyhole; his testimony was corroborated by a woman of questionable reputation who also charged Washington with speaking to her in a familiar manner. Though the jury eventually acquitted Ulrich of assault, messages of support poured in from all over the country during Washington's convalescence; one was an expression of profound regret from the NAACP.

The era of good feelings did not last long. Little basis for real congeniality existed between Washington, on one hand, and Villard and Du Bois, on the other; furthermore, conciliatory words and gestures could not hide the fact that the NAACP had arisen largely as a protest against the Tuskegee type of leadership. As Villard said of Washington's stronger utterances, "They are good enough as far as they go, but they do not go far enough to satisfy a Garrison!" Washington sympathized with some of the NAACP's activities; he heartily approved the test cases carried into the courts, welcomed the campaign against lynching waged by the *Crisis,* and hailed with enthusiasm such victories as the Supreme Court's invalidation of the grandfather clause. But he could never fully approve the methods of "Villard's organization," as he called it, and the NAACP, in turn, could not conceal its impatience with his. Despite continued sniping from Du Bois, Washington went his own way with equanimity, for the challenge of the NAACP was never great enough to shake the foundations of his influence.

X I

"Not in Terms of Race or Color"

WASHINGTON'S activities as a national leader, important as they were, never diverted him from his primary task. His heart was always at Tuskegee. Its phenomenal growth, its duplication throughout the Southern states, and its success in raising economic and moral standards proved the efficacy, for most Negroes of that era, of its founder's educational philosophy. From the first it helped to prepare the Negro, as Washington said it would, for the day when he could press more successfully for complete integration into American life. It was true that industrial education did not provide a complete answer to the Negro's problem; it was also true, as Washington himself realized before his death, that some of his ideas on race relations were obsolescent. But this did not detract from the enduring monument which Tuskegee and its solid achievements represented.

A young teacher who arrived at Tuskegee from Massachusetts in 1904 testified to the impression the school made even on those who tended to discount it. Having been well indoctrinated by the anti-Washington group in Boston, the young instructor could not believe what he saw. Tuskegee "is as far above the Boston criticism as the stars are above the critics," he wrote back to a friend. "The school offers advanced courses equivalent to any high school courses, and the notion that Tuskegee teaches A.B.C.'s is another joke for the Boston joke book. . . . Everybody works and the greatest worker is Mr. B. T. Washington."

The last statement was no exaggeration. As his secretary once observed, Washington was "a task master, a driver, and a relentless critic," but he taxed himself more heavily than he did anyone else. At six o'clock every morning he was out in his barnyard, feeding his prized Berkshires and Poland Chinas (the pig, he maintained, was his favorite animal) or gathering the eggs. "I like to find the new eggs each morning myself, and am selfish enough to permit no one else to do this in my place," he confessed. After breakfast, armed with pencil and notebook, he mounted his gray horse for his morning inspection tour of the campus; by eight o'clock he was at his desk dictating replies to the more than a hundred letters that arrived daily. Despite frequent exhaustion at the end of the day, he would insist on an hour's ride or hunting just before dinner. Like his friend Theodore Roosevelt, he believed in the strenuous life.

Tuskegee was the creation of his own hands, and to the end his touch could be felt in every one of its far-flung departments. Through keen personal observation, departmental reports, and reports from faculty committees or staff members he knew everything that went on and took it upon himself to see that every fault was corrected. If a Sunday School teacher had failed to meet his class, Washington wanted to know why; if the coffee in the dining

hall were lukewarm, he immediately called for the stew-
ard. "Every person employed in the institution," wrote
Scott, "from the most important department heads down to
the men who removed ashes and garbage were [*sic*] under
the stimulating apprehension that his eye might be upon
them at any moment." A teacher who did not measure up
to the desired standard would promptly receive a sharp
note with a specific criticism such as, "Your work yesterday was very far from satisfactory, *not based upon a single
human experience or human activity.*"

Mrs. Washington, who was director of Women's Industries, could claim no special exemption from this vigi-
lance. "The yard of the Practice Cottage does not present
a model appearance by any means," he wrote to her on
one occasion. "So far as I can see, there is not a sign of a
flower or anything like a flower or shrub in the yard." Or
again: "Mrs. Washington. Hereafter when any machines
get out of order please report the matter to Mr. J. H.
Washington as speedily as possible. It is quite a loss to
have six sewing machines not in condition to be used." A
strong-minded person herself, Mrs. Washington often re-
taliated in kind. In reply to his note, "I write to ask, in
case you entertain visitors here during the Conference,
that you arrange, if possible, to serve your dinner only
after the adjournment of the Worker's Conference," she
wrote indignantly, "I never do so at any other time!" Her
only answer to another note was, "Umph! Umph!!
Umph!!!"

Interested only in results, he would sometimes ask three
people to attend to the same matter. Occasionally he
would exasperate a staff member by dictating suggestions
in rapid succession, then calling for results before even one

could be put into effect. Also trying to his subordinates were actions prompted by personal whims or fancies. Though the institution ran on a rigid schedule, Washington would sometimes decree an extra half hour's sleep in the morning or even a half holiday. Completely disregarding teachers' plans, he would order the entire senior class out for a ten-mile trip to see a particularly well-run farm or school. If he returned from an absence to find that his executive council had taken some action with which he did not agree, he would reopen the case and, if he chose, overrule the council's decision. When the faculty refused to graduate one boy, Washington personally ordered him given a diploma as a reward for sticking to his work despite repeated failures.

His penchant for humorous stories and sallies (Scott felt that, as in Lincoln's case, they acted as a safety valve) sometimes led him into difficulties with members of his staff. Like any administrator, he had his share of ruffled feelings to smooth; writing to one teacher who had objected to "the way you attacked me in faculty meeting," Washington explained that he was merely trying to be facetious. Some of the faculty grumbled that the principal treated them as if he were the teacher and they the pupils. Certainly he expected them to toe the line in matters of conduct; as one of them observed, "If any man on this faculty didn't treat his wife well or pay his debt, or gambled or got drunk, he was struck off the Tuskegee pay roll."

Fortunately, this personal rule was tempered by kindness and thoughtfulness. Washington liked nothing better than to send products from his own garden or barnyard to colleagues and friends; he took particular pleasure in special gifts like one he dispatched to a long-time associate in

New York: "I am sending you today, express charges pre-paid," he wrote, "two dressed O'Possums with sweet po-tatoes which I hope you and your friends will enjoy." He used Sunday-morning breakfast as an occasion for personal contact with his teachers, in whom he had a genuine in-terest, and was always ready with a pat on the back for the subordinate whose work pleased him.

Still, the benevolence of Washington's absolutism could not entirely prevent resentment against his methods, and a clique of dissidents arose within the Tuskegee family. G. David Houston, the young instructor from Massachu-setts, joined this group within two years of his arrival and was soon voicing its criticism in letters to friends. "Mr. Washington's scheme," he wrote, "is to have such a control over his teachers that they will tremble at his approach. Most teachers like to see the train puff off with him and dread to hear the engine whistling his return. . . . I must leave here as soon as possible. I positively cannot remain longer under such tyranny."

Reports of Houston's criticism reached Tuskegee only after the young man had left the school, armed with let-ters of recommendation for a position elsewhere. Wash-ington immediately wrote a cool, dispassionate letter warning Houston, then in Boston, that if a satisfactory explanation were not forthcoming, the recommendations would be withdrawn. When Houston admitted his de-fection but stoutly disclaimed any connection with the anti-Tuskegee party in Boston, Washington forgave the bitterly critical personal remarks and even wrote him an-other letter of recommendation.

Whatever the Tuskegee faculty members may have thought of the principal, the students idolized "Mr. B.T."

When the teachers sometimes complained that their welfare was being overlooked, he reminded them that teachers were required only for the benefit of the students, for whom the Institute existed. "That the students should be happy," wrote Scott, "was almost a mania with him." To their delight he would occasionally call a mass meeting for the airing of wrongs, permitting unbridled criticism on which many teachers frowned. A coy letter from one senior class expressed pleasure at the improvement of the food, observing, "It is quite evident that some one has probably extended his influence in this behalf."

A class in psychology which he taught seniors offered him his most intimate contact with students. "It is here," wrote one youth, "that the members of the senior class talk of their past and future lives and receive the outpourings of a great but simple soul." When the faculty committee on curriculum once recommended the elimination of this course, Washington indignantly refused to approve the recommendation. "I like to come into contact with the seniors in this study," he declared. "I like to know the seniors and like to have them know me." He constantly attempted to protect poorer students from embarrassment by resisting the tendency to charge admission fees to various campus functions. When the occasion obviously justified an admission charge, Washington secretly arranged to have needy students admitted at his personal expense.

Undoubtedly remembering his own unimpressive appearance when he arrived at Hampton, he often relied solely on intuition in dealing with students. For example, something in a tough, sullen youth named Jailous Purdue, who arrived at Tuskegee in 1888 at the age of seventeen, caught Washington's interest. "I was a rough, wild boy,"

Purdue himself admitted later, "using bad language and drinking whiskey, and I handed the bottle round to other students." When Purdue threatened with a knife a teacher who had unjustly accused him, Washington did not send the boy away. Gradually, bolstered by the principal's confidence, Purdue began to change. Though he never completed his academic work, he learned the construction trade so well that he became a successful contractor and eventually returned to Tuskegee as an instructor in carpentry.

The students responded warmly and wholeheartedly to Washington's fervent interest in them. As one of them testified, his personality was "the great thing at Tuskegee, and every student who goes there feels the strength of the man's rugged individuality. 'Mr. B.T.' is an affectionate term used by the students, but it springs from an indescribable, spontaneous feeling of love and veneration." He created in his students a spirit of loyalty both to himself and to their school. "Whatever my accomplishments may be, the credit is due to Tuskegee" became a refrain repeated time and again by Tuskegee graduates. "I have not forgotten you, my school, nor my race," wrote one girl in a typical letter. Washington commanded the affection and respect even of students who had not absorbed all the lessons he tried to teach. Writing to one graduate as "father to prodigal son," he refused to recommend the youth because of untrustworthiness; the boy, who signed his letter, "Your beloved friend," answered that he would tread the straight and narrow path from that time on in an attempt to win Washington's confidence.

In part, the loyalty of Tuskegee graduates was a response to the Institute's continuing interest in them. Each year Washington sent out a letter to all alumni encouraging them in whatever they were doing and asking them to send news of themselves back to the Division of Records and Research. In addition, a copy of the *Student* regularly carried news of Tuskegee to every graduate. After Tuskegee had been in existence for some time, Washington had his staff publish a book of individual success stories about Tuskegee graduates which was designed to show the kind of results achieved by industrial education.

Such projects indicated Washington's astute sense of public relations. Having a "nose for a story" which matched that of the best professional newsmen, he was continually suggesting to his staff small items or events which could be turned into good publicity for the school. Though he did not seek personal publicity for its own sake, he realized that his own activities kept Tuskegee in the news; consequently, he cultivated friendly relations with the press and never denied himself to reporters.

He also knew that publicity represented only a small part of public relations. He wrote hundreds of letters weekly to persons who had manifested an interest in the school or whom he wanted to interest. Though Andrew Carnegie eventually became Tuskegee's largest single donor, Washington courted him for ten years before getting any substantial contribution. Washington was not, however, interested only in people who might aid the school financially. He coveted the support of even the most humble people, white and black, and gave generously of his time to them. Often when he was away from Tuskegee on trips, a proud Negro parent would come up to him and say somewhat bashfully, "I 'spec you know my boy — he's down to your school. He's a tall, black boy an' wears a derby hat." On his return to Tuskegee Washington would make it a point to look up the boy and write a personal report to his parents.

He had a weakness for the ne'er-do-wells of his race despite the fact that most of them exemplified traits he generally deplored. He was an easy mark for one such character who rushed out to stop him one day as he drove down the streets of Tuskegee. "I'se got a turkey for yo' Thanksgivin'!" said the old man breathlessly. Washington asked how much the turkey weighed, thanked him warmly, and was about to drive on when his benefactor added, "I jest wants to borrow a dollar for to fatten yo' turkey for you." Washington laughed and handed over the dollar. Among his warmest friends were "Old Man Brannum," the original cook for the school, and Uncle Harry Varner, night watchman of Tuskegee in the early days. When, late in life, Uncle Harry decided to build a house, Washington dug into his own pocket for funds and spent hours helping him select his lot, draw his plans, and supervise construction.

Believing that it was the duty of the fortunate to help the unfortunate, he maintained a contingency fund in the Tuskegee budget to take care of persons like an old woman near the school who was about to be evicted from her home. When some of the older colored people appeared, as they always did, at the annual picnic for the Tuskegee staff, Washington welcomed them as honored guests and allowed them to carry away baskets loaded with provisions. He constantly warned his students that a modicum of education did not give them warrant to look down on their own parents or on the humble members of their race. Before the influx of farmers and their families for the annual Tuskegee Conference, he urged his students to seek out for attention the most poverty-stricken, forlorn, and discouraged people. "In doing that," he told them, "you will do the most for yourselves."

Whether in the company of Tuskegee farmers, wealthy Easterners, or titled heads of Europe, he possessed a remarkable natural poise; humility, self-assurance, and dignity struck a wonderful balance in his temperament. A guest who saw him at Stafford House, home of the Duke of Sutherland, as early as 1899, marveled at his bearing: "There were some people present who were evidently very much impressed by their surroundings. Booker Washington seemed to be absolutely unconscious of the splendor of the house in which he was, or of the society in which for the moment he found himself." On another occasion he was going down a hotel hallway in Des Moines when a woman guest, mistaking him for a porter, asked him for water. Completely unruffled, he went to the desk and had water sent up to her.

This even disposition stood him in good stead when more was at stake. At a meeting held at Tuskegee, Washington had invited a prominent white man, a former Confederate soldier, to speak. Bishop John C. Dancy, a Negro, preceded the speaker, and T. Thomas Fortune was to follow him. Dancy's praise of the New England men and women who had come South after the war infuriated the Confederate veteran, who waved his manuscript and said, "I have written this address for you, but I will not deliver it. I want to give you niggers a few words of plain talk and advice. No such address as you have just listened to is going to do you any good; it's going to spoil you. You had better not listen to such speeches. You might just as well understand that this is a white man's country, as far as the South is concerned, and we are going to make you keep your place. Understand that. I have nothing more to say to you."

Calm, but with his jaw hard set, Washington rose and said to his audience, "I am sure you will agree with me that we have had enough eloquence for one occasion. We shall listen to the next speaker at another occasion, when we are not so fagged out. We will now rise, sing the doxology, and be dismissed."

In part, this exterior calm was deliberately cultivated. Washington did not often let down his guard. In conferences he habitually remained silent, pulling on his pipe (though he never smoked in front of students at Tuskegee), and listening to what others had to say. Despite his apparent indifference to slights or attacks, however, Washington was quite sensitive. One Christmas, after all the presents had been opened, it was evident that his children had neglected to give their father anything. Very much hurt, he called his wife aside and said, "Maggie, they've not given me a single Christmas present!" Mrs. Washington made sure that such a slip did not happen again.

Though he was devoted to his children, only Portia gave him reason for much paternal pride. After training at Bradford Academy and Wellesley, she went to Europe to study music. During her stay there, in letters signed, "Your papa," Washington wrote to her the kind of letters any father might have written to a young girl, sending her money, giving her advice, and warning her not to "overdo." "What you need," he cautioned her, "is plenty of good, quiet rest, not running around." In 1907 Portia married William Sidney Pitman, a young Negro architect who taught at Tuskegee and designed a number of public buildings in the South.

Washington's two sons by no means approached their father in ability or achievement. Young Booker, or Baker, as he was known when he was young, was a problem child who could never apply himself and gave trouble to all who supervised him. His teacher reported him "repeatedly rude and outspoken" as a boy of sixteen. As late as 1914, Washington wrote to a member of his staff under whom Booker was working, "Just as fast as his ability will stand it, I hope you will give Booker something to do every day that will enable him to use his own judgment or initiative." His second son, Davidson Washington, served in several minor capacities at Tuskegee. For some years he represented the Institute as Northern financial agent; later he joined the public-relations staff as official receptionist to the thousands of visitors to the campus.

One of these visitors to Tuskegee soon after the turn of the century was asked on his return if he had seen Booker T. Washington's school. "School!" he replied. "I have seen Booker T. Washington's city." What was true then was even more true at the time Washington died in 1915. Tuskegee's handsome two-million-dollar plant, with its massive brick buildings, neatly landscaped grounds, up-to-date shops and barns, and twenty-four hundred acres of farmland, was worth the time of any tourist. Almost two thousand young men and women, neatly uniformed in blue and white, were enrolled as regular students, while special courses and extension work raised the total number of those receiving instruction to almost four thousand. Daughter institutions, founded and directed by Tuskegee graduates, dotted the map of the Southern states. Even Washington's critics paid tribute to his achievement; but increasingly toward the end of his long ascendancy in Negro affairs, other members of his race began to agree with the NAACP that Washington's program could not, of itself, prevent discrimination and achieve full citizenship.

Washington himself, realizing that discrimination was mounting in many areas despite the Negro's economic and cultural advancement, moved toward a stronger position on civil rights during the last few years of his life. He had always defended the Negro's right to enter complaints "in a conservative and sensible manner," but later his own utterances became less and less conservative. "I am not deceived," he stated emphatically to the National Colored Teachers' Association in 1911. "I do not overlook the wrongs that often perplex and embarrass us in this country. I condemn with all the strength of my nature the barbarous habit of lynching a human being, whether black or white, without legal trial. I condemn any practice in any state that results in not enforcing the law with a certainty and justice, regardless of race or color." A year later, his article for the *Century* magazine entitled, "Is the Negro Having a Fair Chance?" left no doubt that the answer was, "No."

This shift was perceptible all along the line. Discrimination in public education particularly galled him. As early as 1905, his interest in this question had prompted him to ask Villard to publicize one situation in which the Negro's share of state funds for education amounted to a startlingly small fraction of the amount allotted to whites. "As no color line is drawn in the courts in the matter of punishing crime," he said, "neither should any color line be drawn in the opportunity to get education in the public schools." Over and over again he condemned the inequity in state appropriations for whites and Negroes, pointing out that in some instances more money was paid for the labor of Negro convicts under the convict lease system than for Negro teachers.

As he grew older, his willingness to abide by Southern custom became somewhat frayed. On one occasion he went onto the stage of a theater in Tampa to speak, only to find that Negroes and whites in the audience had been separated by a row of sheets hung down the aisle. Visibly annoyed, he said without a word of introduction or greeting, "I have traveled all over this country and in many foreign lands, but this is the first time that I have ever seen white people and colored people separated by sheets. Now, before I begin my remarks, I want that thing taken down from there." When the sheets came down, he went on with his speech.

He had just as little patience with the residential segregation laws which were going into effect all over the South. "You cannot help the Negro very much and you do not help the white man very much by yielding to the temptation of trying to shut the race off in certain segregated parts of American cities," he told a Battle Creek audience in 1914. Such legislation, he declared, was not only unnecessary, but unjust. "Every thoughtful Negro" resented a segregated system, because his people never got equal health facilities, lighting, cleanliness, police protection, or the use of public services like libraries and hospitals — though they were compelled to pay taxes on the same basis as the whites. The Negro knew, he said in a prophetic phrase, that segregation meant "an unfair deal."

He also inveighed against discrimination in travel accommodations and did his best to hold railroad companies to the spirit and letter of the "separate but equal" principle. His approach, as always, was reasonable. He urged Negroes, for example, to keep themselves clean and neat while traveling so as to remove any grounds for criticism. But on "Railroad Days," which he organized through the Negro Business League, he also urged Negro patrons to lay before railroad-company officials specific abuses and suggestions for improvement.

That Southern justice made the Negro consider the courts places of punishment rather than protection also disturbed him. He sent to the press articles asking jury representation for Negroes and spoke out against the practice of "arresting so many of our people for petty and trivial offenses." The convict lease system, under which prisoners were hired out to persons who cared little that they were human beings — a custom which opened the way to flagrant abuse of Negroes in particular — drew Washington's fire. He also protested against another form of slavery, the peonage permitted by Southern contract-labor laws. Since economic independence for the Negro farmer had always been one of his central objectives, he considered the Supreme Court decision of 1911, voiding the labor law of Alabama, "the most important national event that has occurred within recent years."

Above all he continued to hammer at lynching. Though he rarely failed to point out that progress was being made (the number of lychings per year had been decreasing slowly since 1892), he did not fail to condemn where condemnation was due. By coincidence he happened to be speaking in Jacksonville, Florida, shortly after a murder had been committed by two Negroes. Washington refused to cancel the engagement; instead he delivered a strong denunciation of lynching to the accompaniment of shouts from a would-be lynch mob on its way to the prison nearby.

The round-the-clock pattern of his life, consisting as it did of incessant speechmaking, punctuated by constant traveling and intervals at Tuskegee, would have been enough to break the health of even a younger man. When, during his last years, he contracted diabetes, he could no longer safely maintain his usual pace. Still, he refused to slow down. The year 1914 found him occupied, as usual, with everything from the purchase of more land and changes in staff personnel to the condition of the poultry and the means of adding a profitable butter-making industry to the trade courses at Tuskegee. As usual, too, he was adding to the physical plant: a large central-heating and power plant was going up during the same year.

Money was still a problem, for he had overspent his 1913 budget and did not have the funds to pay for the heating plant. "When we get out of this hole," Washington wrote to one of his trustees, "I think we ought to be very careful about getting into another one." To meet the deficit he organized his last fund-raising campaign in the late spring of 1915, sending into the North and West five workers who reported to him by wire daily and to whom he constantly fired letters of instruction. After the successful close of the campaign he set out on what had come to be a normal summer's schedule. He spoke at Meadville, Pennsylvania, and Worcester, Massachusetts, attended the inauguration of the president of Tufts College, then headed to New York for meetings of both the Tuskegee and Fisk trustees. After a series of lectures at the summer school in

Tuskegee, he returned to New York for a meeting of the executive committee of the Jeanes Fund. The Fourth of July found him speaking in Atlanta, after which he went to Illinois for a week of addresses on the Chautauqua circuit. From a second Chautauqua tour in Iowa, Kansas, and Nebraska, he went to Nova Scotia, speaking at Wooster, Ohio, on the way. Toward the end of August he was back in Boston to preside at the Fifteenth Anniversary meeting of the Business League.

Scott and his more intimate associates, noticing in Boston that Washington had nearly reached the breaking point, persuaded him to spend the last two weeks of September on a fishing trip. Feeling rested (nothing relaxed him so much as fishing), he plunged again into his accustomed schedule of activity. Leaving Tuskegee on October 23, he spoke in New Haven on October 25. Back in New York, he finally collapsed and was taken to St. Luke's Hospital by members of his board. According to the doctors there, he was suffering from complete nervous exhaustion and arteriosclerosis; as one of them said, it was "uncanny to see a man up and about who ought by all the laws of nature to be dead."

When told that he could not live much longer, he asked to go home. "I was born in the South, I have lived and labored in the South, and I expect to die and be buried in the South," he insisted in a widely publicized statement. Defying the doctor's warning that he could not survive the trip, he boarded the train and held onto life by the strength of his will. With Mrs. Washington at his side, he arrived at Tuskegee on the evening of November 13, apparently a little stronger, and happy in the knowledge that he had reached home. He died the next morning.

To a generation of white Americans who had never known any Negro leader other than Booker T. Washington, his death left a curious void in the accepted pattern of thinking about race problems. In the hearts and minds of the vast majority of his own race as well, there was no one to replace him. Still, the end of his personal leadership did pave the way for the kind of harmony for which Washington himself had so often spoken. "We must have a united race," he had said in one of his last words of advice to Negroes. "We must have men big enough and broad enough . . . to lay aside all personal differences, all petty jealousies," men "who are willing to lay their lives upon the altar of our race's welfare as a sacrifice." Less impatient at the end with what he termed "abstract" protest, he recognized that organizations of all kinds — "the religious, the educational, the political, the literary, the secret and fraternal bodies, as well as those that deal with the civil rights of our people" — had to work together to solve the Negro's complex problem.

General agreement on the principles to be emphasized in a co-operative program for race advancement came about through a conference of distinguished Negro leaders held near Amenia, New York, the year after Washington's death. One in their desire to forget old factional alignments and promote racial unity, the delegates agreed to encourage all forms of education for the Negro, work for his enfranchisement, and to recognize special circumstances affecting Negro work in the South. They openly accepted as their goal complete and unqualified integration of the Negro into American society.

This had been Washington's goal as well, but realizing that the Negro could do little at that time to block the current of discrimination, he had put his emphasis on the practical and the possible. Like a seasoned boxer, he never took the full force of his opponent's attack, but rolled with the punch, attempting to protect himself and his race for more effective battles later. His policy was distinctly realistic. He began by looking at his race with a critical and remarkably objective eye, admitting the prevalence of ignorance, immorality, and irresponsibility; thereby he disarmed his white listeners and gave logic and common sense to his proposed remedies.

His strategy was just as realistic as his estimate of the situation. "I do not deny," he wrote, "that I was frequently tempted, during the early years of my work, to join in the denunciation of the evils and injustice that I saw about me. But when I thought the matter over, I saw that such a course would accomplish no good and that it would do a great deal of harm." Washington believed that his alternative approach was not only constructive but aggressive. "I felt that the millions of Negroes needed something more than to be reminded of their sufferings and of their political rights, that they needed to do more than defend themselves," he explained. For obvious reasons the average Southern Negro could take no part in agitation or protest; he could only vaguely hope that he or his children might eventually benefit from efforts carried on in his behalf by men far removed from his day-to-day existence. But Washington fired the imagination of even the poorest tenant farmer by offering him an active role in a creative, dynamic program which affected him personally and directly. By setting tangible goals and demonstrating how they could be reached, he pointed the way to a better life for the Negro in his own home and community. Furthermore, a wealth of evidence existed to show that the program got results which were understandable and real.

The really new element in Washington's program was his emphasis on economic independence and security. Here he was making a decided break with the past, and part of the opposition to him sprang from the unwillingness of many "radicals" to give up traditional political remedies as the exclusive means to race advancement. Many did not recognize, as Washington did, that the color line was being redrawn to exclude Negroes from occupations which had been theirs by custom. Washington correctly concluded that many Negroes considered economic opportunity more essential than the ballot, social equality, or other objectives of those who pinned their faith primarily on protest. In his struggle to keep the door of economic opportunity open, he was fighting for an objective closely related to that of "Fair Employment Practices" legislation more than a quarter of a century later.

By overemphasizing industrial education, he highlighted the fact that economic progress offered a means to full integration no less important than political means, and that the two complemented each other. Furthermore, by schooling his race in such traditional American virtues as hard work, thrift, integrity, responsibility, and initiative, he helped Negroes forge a common bond with their white neighbors. His predecessors had taken their lead from Thomas Jefferson. Washington took his from Benjamin Franklin, and by doing so, introduced a strain into the Negro's Americanism which strengthened his claim to full citizenship.

Unfortunately, his economic emphasis had its weaknesses as well as its strength. His accurate judgment that the Negro's economic ills contributed to his vulnerability in other areas was partly offset by the fact that he conceived of economics in terms more valid for Franklin's day than for the twentieth century. Though he accurately forecast that for many years the vast majority of Negroes would have to train themselves for the basic occupations, he did not foresee developments which were to alter drastically the nature of these industries. In the first place, he had geared his program to the training of craftsmen and small entrepreneurs, whereas twentieth-century industry demanded labor for the mass-production jobs of the assembly line. In the second place, he failed to see that mechanical farming and consolidation were fast eliminating the necessity for the large agricultural labor force which he had considered a constant in the economic equation, and that the urban migration of Negroes which he so heartily disapproved was only part of a general population shift from farm to city. Still, the later adjustment of Tuskegee and other industrial schools to the needs of a new era showed that these weaknesses could be overcome.

Of more serious consequence were two assumptions on which he based his hope for the elimination of discrimination. He believed, first, that successful competition with whites in the economic realm would raise the Negro in the estimation of the white man and thereby break down prejudice. Experience was to prove just the opposite, especially among the large group of white people closest to the Negro in the social and economic scale.

He also assumed, optimistically, that the tendency of the "best" white people to treat Negroes differently depending on their education, character, and general merit would continue. This tendency, which had allowed a successful Negro like Lewis Adams to command the respect of the entire Tuskegee community, led Washington to believe that the problem of race would be solved as the number of Lewis Adamses could be multiplied. When the advent of discriminatory laws lumped all Negroes together regardless of individual merit, Washington's faith in "progress" made him continue to insist, even while he spoke out more sharply against discrimination, that race relations were steadily improving.

Perhaps the most justified criticism is that Washington's monopoly of leadership prevented those with a different point of view from working effectively in their own way while he continued to work in his. Since the nature of his program and his method of carrying it out kept him from emphasizing complete integration forcefully or in sufficiently specific terms, it was desirable that others do so in order to keep before coming generations of Negroes an ideal and a hope for the future. The rallying to this standard immediately after Washington's death showed that his strong influence had at least to some extent stood in the way of this self-assertion.

Still, most of Washington's weaknesses must be qualified. It is difficult, for example, to condemn him for faith in his fellow man; yet one of the flaws in his program was the fact that it relied too heavily on the co-operation and enlightenment of the Negro's white neighbor. Washington realized that he was taking a chance. "Much will depend," he wrote, "upon the sense of justice which can be kept alive in the breast of the American people." Had white Americans, and particularly white Southerners, been willing to carry out their part of the bargain which Washington offered at Atlanta in 1895, their continuing plea for gradualism would have carried more weight. Instead, only when faced with threatened elimination of the entire segregation system half a century later did most Southern states hasten to implement the "separate but equal" principle to which they had so long paid lip service.

If the years did not fully justify Washington's faith in the white man, what of his faith in his own race? He said many times that he was proud of being a Negro, and that he would not exchange the Negro's future for the future of any race on earth. By mid-century, thirty-five years after Washington's death, the Negro had by no means reached the promised land. Still denied opportunities in many areas of American life, he had earned a name for himself in the fields of entertainment, athletics, and the arts, but had produced only a few men and women of national stature in such areas as statecraft, industry, scholarship, and law. In Washington's phrase, the Negro was still passing through the "severe American crucible." But obvious cracks were appearing in the walls of prejudice and discrimination, and by 1950 the Negro could hope with more realism than at any time since emancipation for the day of liberty and justice for all.

That Booker T. Washington looked forward to this day cannot be doubted; he accepted half a loaf, not as a permanent settlement, but as a means toward obtaining the whole loaf later. To criticize his methods is to make the facile assumption that he had some choice in the matter. He did what was possible, given the time and place in which he lived, and did it to the utmost.

Furthermore, had he offered nothing in the way of precept, he would still have given a great deal by example. He practiced what he preached: courage, self-reliance, integrity, humility, dignity, and consideration for his fellow man. Completely free from race prejudice, he had the ability to lift himself above the level of petty hatreds and selfish ambition. "More and more," he said late in his life, "we must learn to think not in terms of race or color or language or religion or political boundaries, but in terms of humanity." Such vision belonged not to the past, but to the future. In an age which was just beginning to learn that the color of a man's skin has nothing to do with his potential contribution to society, the entire human family benefited from the life of such a man as Booker T. Washington.

A Note on the Sources

THOUGH THE Atlanta Exposition address of 1895 first gave Booker T. Washington national prominence, his autobiography, *Up From Slavery* (1901), spread the story of Tuskegee Institute and its founder all over the globe. This phenomenal best seller remains the principal source for information about Washington's early life. Much of this material, with minor variations, appears in the little-known *The Story of My Life and Work* (1900), an earlier attempt at an autobiography published at about the same time that *Up From Slavery* began appearing serially in the *Outlook* magazine. Unlike the simple, direct *Up From Slavery, The Story of My Life and Work* is a rambling assortment of recollections, anecdotes, and speeches, connected by a thin thread of personal narrative.

Working with the Hands (1904) and *Tuskegee and Its People* (1905) tell more of the Tuskegee story, with particular emphasis on the development and achievements of industrial education. To a large extent, however, Washington's published works deal with the broader problem of race relations. He elaborated his views in *The Future of the American Negro* (1899), *My Larger Education* (1911), which is partly autobiographical, and in contributions to joint works such as *The Negro Problem* (1903) and *The Negro in the South* (1907). In addition, he turned out, with the aid of his research staff, a steady flow of articles for periodicals. Some of these, like "The Negro and the Labor Unions" (*Atlantic Monthly,* 1913) and "Is the Negro Having a Fair Chance?" (*Century Magazine,* 1912), give significant insight into the thinking of his mature years.

Other books published over his name show rather obviously the hands of outside researchers and writers. Washington's biography of Frederick Douglass (1907) was largely written by his friend S. Laing Williams, while Robert E. Park did most of the work on *The Story of the Negro* (1909) and *The Man Farthest Down* (1912). The latter is a summary of Washington's experiences and observations in Europe. *The Negro in Business* (1907) is a catalogue of Negro achievement in the commercial world designed to build race pride by citing successful Negro entrepreneurs as examples to Negro youth.

The thousands of speeches Washington delivered during his lifetime constitute a fertile source for his ideas. After Washington's death his youngest son, E. Davidson Washington, collected a number of the most significant public utterances in a volume entitled *Selected Speeches* (1932). In addition, the press of the day covered most of the major addresses and hundreds of the minor ones. Such little books as *Putting the Most into Life* and *Character Building,* which are collections of the Sunday-evening talks to his students at Tuskegee, reflect Washington's faith in traditional American virtues.

By far the largest additional source of information about Washington, as yet largely untapped, is the mass of Booker T. Washington Papers in the Library of Congress. This vast collection, crammed into some two thousand file boxes in a semiorganized fashion, awaits systematic examination and cataloguing before it can be used effectively. Even so, the Papers are rewarding, not only for additional information, but for glimpses of Washington as he was when, in rare instances, he let down his guard; they indicate that Washington as his closest friends knew him was essentially the same man he was believed to be on the basis of public knowledge. Of particular interest is his correspondence with such persons as Theodore Roosevelt, William Howard Taft, William E. B. Du Bois, George Washington Carver, and Oswald Garrison Villard; even more revealing are the letters to little-known but intimate friends such as S. Laing Williams, Whitefield McKinlay, Charles W. Anderson, and Charles Banks. For a discussion of the Washington Papers, see Franklin Frazier's article in *The Library of Congress Quarterly Journal of Acquisitions,* February 1945, II, pp. 23–31.

Possibly because of the immediate and continuing success of *Up From Slavery,* few writers have attempted full-length biographies of Washington. *Booker T. Washington: Builder of a Civilization* (1916), written by Emmett Scott and Lyman Beecher Stowe, is, as would be expected, uncritical, but it contains valuable information and some fairly frank admissions about Washington's characteristics and methods. Such works as Frederick S. Drinker's *Booker T. Washington: The Master Mind of a Child of Slavery* (1915), Benjamin F. Riley's *The Life and Times of Booker T. Washington* (1916), and, later, Theodore Sylvester Boone's *The Philosophy of Booker T. Washington, the Apostle of Progress, the Pioneer of the New Deal* (1939) are of little value. The best biography to date is Basil

Mathews's *Booker T. Washington, Educator and Interracial Interpreter* (1948). Mathews's book quite frankly is written by a Washington admirer with the approval of the authorities at Tuskegee, but it is the product of much painstaking research, and its good points outweigh its shortcomings.

The press, including specifically the Negro press, is a valuable source, particularly for its study of the opposition to Washington. The clipping books in the Washington Papers contain thousands of press notices. W. E. B. Du Bois, leader of the opposition during Washington's lifetime, has provided much of the information about those who did not agree with the Tuskegee approach; the *Crisis*, which he began to edit in 1910, deserves special mention, as does Du Bois's autobiographical *Dusk of Dawn* (1940). General works of special value for background material are Gunnar Myrdal's *An American Dilemma* (1944), John Hope Franklin's *From Slavery to Freedom* (1947), and C. Vann Woodward's *Origins of the New South* (1951).

Index